CW00346204

How to Be Angry

of related interest

Little Volcanoes
Helping Young Children to Deal with Angry Feelings
Warwick Pudney and Éliane Whitehouse
ISBN 978 1 84905 217 7

Anger Management Games for Children
Deborah M. Plummer
Illustrated by Jane Serrurier
ISBN 978 1 84310 628 9

Working with Anger and Young People
Nick Luxmoore
ISBN 978 1 84310 466 7

Helping Children to Cope with Change, Stress and Anxiety
A Photocopiable Activities Book
Deborah M. Plummer
Illustrated by Alice Harper
ISBN 978 1 84310 960 0

Growing Young Leaders
Working with Young People at Risk of Violence
Jo Broadwood and Nic Fine
ISBN 978 1 84905 183 5

Games and Activities for Exploring Feelings
Vanessa Rogers
ISBN 978 1 84905 222 1

Cyberbullying
Activities to Help Children and Teens to Stay Safe in a Texting,
Twittering, Social Networking World
Vanessa Rogers
ISBN 978 1 84905 105 7

Playing with Fire
Training for Those Working with Young People in Conflict
Fiona Macbeth and Nic Fine with Jo Broadwood, Carey Haslam and Nik Pitcher
ISBN 978 1 84905 184 2

How to Be Angry

An Assertive Anger Expression Group Guide for Kids and Teens

Signe Whitson

Foreword by Dr. Nicholas J. Long

Jessica Kingsley *Publishers*
London and Philadelphia

Definitions from Long, Long and Whitson 2009 on p.44 and pp.58–59
are reproduced by permission of PRO-ED, Inc.

First published in 2011
by Jessica Kingsley Publishers
116 Pentonville Road
London N1 9JB, UK
and
400 Market Street, Suite 400
Philadelphia, PA 19106, USA

www.jkp.com

Copyright © Signe Whitson 2011
Foreword copyright © Nicholas J. Long 2011

All rights reserved. No part of this publication may be reproduced in any material form (including photocopying of any pages other than those marked with a ✓, storing it in any medium by electronic means and whether or not transiently or incidentally to some other use of this publication) without the written permission of the copyright owner except in accordance with the provisions of the Copyright, Designs and Patents Act 1988 or under the terms of a licence issued by the Copyright Licensing Agency Ltd, Saffron House, 6–10 Kirby Street, London EC1N 8TS. Applications for the copyright owner's written permission to reproduce any part of this publication should be addressed to the publisher.

Warning: The doing of an unauthorized act in relation to a copyright work
may result in both a civil claim for damages and criminal prosecution.

All pages marked may be photocopied for personal use with this program, but may not
be reproduced for any other purposes without the permission of the publisher.

Library of Congress Cataloging in Publication Data
Whitson, Signe.
  How to be angry : a 15-session assertive anger expression group guide for
kids and teens / Signe Whitson, Nicholas J. Long.
    p. cm.
  Includes bibliographical references.
  ISBN 978-1-84905-867-4 (alk. paper)
  1. Anger in children. 2. Anger in adolescence. 3. Assertiveness in
children. 4. Assertiveness in adolescence. I. Long, Nicholas James, 1929-
II. Title.
  BF723.A4W45 2011
  155.4'1247--dc22

                                    2010052924

British Library Cataloguing in Publication Data
A CIP catalogue record for this book is available from the British Library

ISBN 978 1 84905 867 4

Printed and bound in the United States

For Hannah and Elle:

I love you any way you feel, no matter what you do.

I love you because you are you.

Do not teach your children never to be angry;
teach them how to be angry.

Lyman Abbott

Contents

Part I: Exploring Anger Behaviors

Part II: Developing Assertive Anger Expression Skills

Part III: Committing to Assertive Anger Expression

Foreword

As a developmental psychologist for more than 50 years I have witnessed again and again the destructive effects that ill-expressed anger has on children, in our homes, our schools, and throughout our communities.

From a historical perspective the decision to attack a foe or to run away and wait for a better day kept human beings alive. Aggressive and escape behaviors paid off, landing humans at top of the food chain. As city-states developed and people had to live together in interdependent ways, however, aggressive behaviors had to be curbed. Laws were written and aggressors were tried and punished.

Centuries have passed and every aspect of life has changed, but the bell of progress has not yet rung on replacing old ways of controlling anger in children and youth. Our juvenile courts and treatment centers are bulging with aggressive youth who lack self-control skills. Our schools have too many bullies who intimidate their classmates, and classmates who are not sure how to protect themselves. Too many homes are fraught with conflict between parents who never learned to manage their emotions and their children who follow in their destructive pathway.

Today's young people need specific skills to be able to identify the behaviors that trigger their anger, learn to accept their angry feelings as normal, and to express their anger in assertive, non-hurtful ways. It is a complicated process.

After reading the 15 sessions of this assertive anger expression guide, I am convinced this group curriculum is the answer. *How to Be Angry* is theoretically sound, psychologically realistic, and engagingly interactive. It fills a growing need for educators, social workers, mental health counselors, parents, and other helping adults who face the simultaneous task of affirming the normal experience of anger in the lives of young people while also teaching them how to express this anger effectively, using assertive, relationship-building skills. *How to Be Angry* is the only available resource that combines anger management and assertiveness training skills into one complete and ready-to-use group curriculum for kids who range in age from 5 to 18.

I like the fact that the structured curriculum and solution-focused activities are designed for use with children and youth across a wide age span and in many different types of settings. Each session of *How to Be Angry* features "Suggestions for customizing the curriculum," which provides group facilitators with ideas for adjusting activities, discussions, and journal topics to the age, ability, interests, and developmental needs of group participants. Likewise, each session offers a dedicated *Notes for parents* section that provides discussion-starters and advice for parents who want to extend their child's learning experience beyond the group or adapt the lessons for one-on-one instruction.

The complete, step-by-step instructional guide for group leaders makes it a ready-to-use program:

The first five sessions provide group participants with the basic diagnostic concepts of anger, including identifying common anger triggers and behaviors, emphasizing personal choice in anger expression, exploring the psychology of passive aggression, and using a creative, "right-brain" activity to help young people gain insight into the dynamic struggle between public faces and private realities. The section ends with a session on the role of body language and tone of voice in assertive anger expression.

The second part of the curriculum provides group members with eight solution-focused, real-world skills for assertive anger expression, including using "I-Messages," disagreeing without arguing, making and refusing requests, and, best of all, finding win-win resolutions to interpersonal conflicts. What's more, *How to Be Angry* features two sessions on one of the country's top stressors for kids: bullying. Kids learn how to recognize bullying in all of its forms, from obvious physical aggression to more covert forms of relational aggression, including social exclusion and cyber-bullying. Group members also learn and practice four rules for using assertive skills to stand up to bullies.

In the last two sessions of the curriculum group members have the opportunity to review behaviors that represent four choices in anger expression and make a commitment to replace old patterns with new skills. Kids benefit from learning how to transfer the skills learned in group into their daily interpersonal relationships and gain a sense of accomplishment at successfully completing the group experience.

Signe Whitson needs to be congratulated for developing this innovative and much-needed curriculum for helping children and youth develop positive ways of expressing their feelings of anger.

Anyone working or living with young people will be interested in *How to Be Angry* for the practical guidelines and engaging activities it uses to teach positive choices in anger expression and real-world skills for assertive communication. I can assure you that after teaching this curriculum and experiencing the rewarding comments of the students, this book, *How to Be Angry*, will never be returned to your bookshelf.

Nicholas J. Long PhD,
Professor Emeritus, American University,
President of the Life Space Crisis Intervention Institute—www.lsci.org

Introduction

About this book

Have you ever been in a situation where you were so overwhelmed with feelings of anger that you were at a loss for words? You had the presence of mind to know all of the things that you shouldn't say, but weren't quite sure how to express your true feelings without damaging your relationship. Adults often struggle with effectively communicating their angry feelings. For children, this challenge is doubly difficult; kids don't want to get in trouble for expressing themselves aggressively, but they often lack the skills for communicating assertively.

How to Be Angry: An Assertive Anger Expression Group Guide for Kids and Teens provides a roadmap for educators, counselors, social workers, youth care professionals, and parents to steer children, tweens, and teens through the convoluted pathways of assertive anger expression. Each detailed session in *How to Be Angry*'s complete curriculum provides step-by-step guidelines for leading small groups of kids through specific anger management and assertive emotional expression skills. Participants will learn specific skills such as:

- using I-Messages
- standing up to bullies
- disagreeing without arguing
- making and refusing requests
- responding to anger
- finding win–win solutions.

Engaging, hands-on activities and discussions are customized for children ages 5–18 in school, treatment, recreational and even home settings, and will help youth reflect on important topics such as:

- personal anger styles (aggression, passive aggression, passivity, and assertiveness)
- choices in anger expression
- public faces vs. private realities
- body language and tone of voice
- replacing self-defeating patterns and committing to assertive behaviors.

From the time they are toddlers, children are often coaxed by adults to hide their feelings of anger behind a social smile. Worse yet, kids hear the explicit message, "Don't be angry," and are actively encouraged to deny this most basic of human emotions. When they act out—either through the tantrums of their earliest years or the rebellion of their teenage ones—they are chastened for all of the behaviors that adults do not want them to use. The lessons in this group curriculum flip this traditional approach. Rather that hammering away at all of the things kids should not do when it comes to expressing their anger, the skill-building activities and discussions in this book provide instruction for kids on *how to be angry effectively*, using assertive behaviors to confront and manage real-life situations.

Who is *How to Be Angry* for?

While anger is a basic human emotion and experienced universally across all ages, races, and cultures, skills for assertive anger expression do not come naturally to most. Rather, learning how to make positive choices in expressing anger is a step-by-step process for young people.

Anyone living or working with young people will be interested in *How to Be Angry* for the practical guidelines and engaging activities it uses to teach positive choices in anger expression and real-world skills for assertive communication.

Education professionals

The 15-session curriculum is written for teachers, school social workers, guidance counselors, and school crisis personnel to help students cope with everyday sources of anger and develop assertive skills to express feelings in ways that do not disrupt the learning environment.

Mental health professionals

Clinical social workers, psychologists, and licensed professional counselors employed in residential youth care, group homes, outpatient, and other mental health settings will be interested in *How to Be Angry* as a complete, ready-to-use 15-week group guide that offers specific objectives and detailed lesson plans for working with youth who struggle with anger control and who are learning skills for assertive self-expression.

Parents and caregivers

Parents and caregivers will also benefit from the lessons of *How to Be Angry*. As primary role models and change agents in the lives of their children, it is essential that parents understand the goals of constructive anger expression and can role model assertive techniques in the home. Each session of the *How to Be Angry* curriculum features a special *Notes for parents* section. Ideas for real-world discussions and at-home conversation starters help parents pick up where group discussions leave off in facilitating constructive change and lasting anger management skills in a young person. For parents whose children are not involved in a *How to Be Angry* group, the *Notes for parents* section provides ideas for adaptation for one-on-one, parent–child discussions.

Helping adults

Anytime that helping adults interact with kids, there is a need for skill-building in effective anger expression. Leaders of afterschool programs, scouting groups, youth-oriented community groups, sports teams, and religious organizations will all find relevant activities and thought-provoking discussions in the *How to Be Angry* curriculum.

Kids!

Most of all, this 15-session group curriculum is designed to teach child and adolescent students and clients valuable skills for effective anger expression and assertive behaviors. The solution-focused lessons, engaging group activities and relevant discussions in this group are designed to help kids overcome self-defeating anger expression patterns (passive, aggressive, and passive aggressive) and adopt skills for assertive self-expression.

The discussions and activities in *How to Be Angry* are designed to be used across a broad span of ages and abilities. There will likely be instances in which certain individuals are able to move quickly through concepts while others may need more focus and explanation. Since this is designed as a group experience, the facilitator will be called upon to use his skill to make the material meaningful for all.

Discussions, activities, handouts, and weekly journal topics are written at the upper-elementary and middle-school level (ages 8–13), though each session has a special "Suggestions for customizing the curriculum" section that provides notes on adapting the lessons for participants of varying ages and abilities. *How to Be Angry* activities have been used with groups of children from kindergarten age through high school students (ages 5–18), in both urban and rural settings. Students rate the activities as "fun" and "interesting" and agree that "now I know what to do when I get angry."

Facilitator qualifications

How to Be Angry is written as a step-by-step facilitation guide so that any adult with professional training in teaching and/or working with young people may lead the group. Facilitators of all experience levels should be sure to thoroughly read the entire curriculum before beginning the group and should review and prepare the materials for each session individually before a group is held. Newcomers to group facilitation will benefit from co-leading the session with another adult to observe and learn the finer points of group process.

Please note: The same adult(s) should facilitate the group session after session. The group process will be less effective if different adults lead the different sessions. Both continuity and the sense of group cohesion are compromised when leadership is inconsistent.

Creating a positive group environment

Children and adolescents do some of their very best learning within small groups. Research shows that positive group environments build resilience in young people by meeting universal needs for attachment, achievement, and belonging (Brendtro, Mitchell and McCall 2009). When kids are able to discuss anger triggers, explore choices for anger expression, and learn skills for assertive self-expression within a supportive group setting, they have the additional benefit of knowing they are not alone. Rather, they feel supported by peers who are "all-in-the-same-boat" (Shulman 2008) and profit from practicing new skills on real-world peers.

The facilitator can help create a positive group environment by:

- role modeling assertive behaviors in all interactions with group members

- demonstrating unconditional positive regard for each participant

- conveying a belief in the abilities and skills of individual members and the group as a whole

- customizing the curriculum to the needs of the group

- encouraging active participation

- providing regular feedback to individual members and on group activities

- fostering trust

- safeguarding participants from hurtful interactions

- asking group members for their opinions and feedback

- celebrating group learning and successes.

Early on in the group formation, pay particular attention to icebreaker activities and discussion opportunities that help participants bond with one another and develop trusting, supportive relationships. Take an active role in assigning participants to different pairings or small groups each session, to avoid the formation of cliques within the group or feelings of exclusion for individual members. The more group members develop the belief that they are "all in it together," the more productive the learning environment will be.

Using the curriculum

How to Be Angry is a complete, ready-to-use curriculum. Each session begins by outlining specific learning objectives for participants and provides a list of necessary materials and *Before beginning* preparations.

Detailed, step-by-step instructions are provided to the facilitator for each session, along with italicized suggestions for general wording and important messages to convey to participants. Following the instructions for each session, facilitators will find handouts, activity templates, and weekly journal pages that can be photocopied and distributed to group participants.

Several of the sessions utilize role-plays, scenarios, questions, and/or sentence-starters pre-printed on index cards, for distribution to participants. It may be helpful for the facilitator to prepare extra cards in order to customize the activities with relevant real-world examples and provide a variety of options that encourage maximum participation from group members.

Time requirements

Each session is designed to be completed in about an hour, though this time frame is offered only as a guideline. Depending on the program schedule, the day, the group, and the mood (among other variables), some discussions will need more or less time. Sessions can be divided and continued at later points, especially for younger participants who need additional time to learn and process new information or when intense sharing occurs (e.g. during the sessions on Keeping Bullies at Bay.) Skills that require extra practice (e.g. *Using I-Messages*) may also necessitate additional time. The facilitator should use discretion in guiding the group through each lesson, taking care to make the atmosphere interesting and fun and, most importantly, allowing each child to feel heard and understood.

Scheduling

Whenever possible, schedule the group sessions at regular intervals. Kids benefit from the predictability of knowing when sessions will take place and come to look forward to the regular interactions. Also, avoid holding the *How to Be Angry* sessions during times of day when participants will be likely to have to come and go or miss frequent sessions. It is frustrating for young people to begin addressing a topic but not have the opportunity to finish it and it is disruptive to the group process for the membership to be inconsistent. When adults prioritize group time, they signal to participants that the curriculum is important and convey their commitment to participants' learning.

The group room

Along with dedicating regular time to the group, it is helpful to select a physical space that accommodates group members comfortably and allows enough space for movement around the room during group activities. Additionally, it is important to use a room that is free of noisy distractions and provides enough privacy for participants to feel safe engaging in honest self-reflection and discussion.

Group size

Because each session is built largely around group activities and discussions, the ideal group size is 8–10 kids per adult facilitator. Whenever possible, enough adults should be present to allow each of the participants the chance to feel heard and understood and to be sure that all concerns, questions, and issues receive due attention.

Group materials

Most of the *How to Be Angry* sessions involve handouts that are completed during group, though they also serve as helpful "take home" reminders of specific skills. Every group session suggests a weekly journal topic for participants to continue their reflection outside the group. It is helpful to provide participants with a folder in which they can keep all of their *How to Be Angry* papers.

Feedback

I am interested in your feedback! After leading group sessions, please forward comments to me via www.signewhitson.com.

Part I
Exploring Anger Behaviors

That Makes Me So Mad!
Identifying Common Anger Triggers

Session objectives

- To introduce the purpose of the *How to Be Angry* group and preview the learning that will occur.

- To set the tone for an engaging, practical, respectful and fun group experience.

- To define "anger" and normalize the experience of anger in our daily lives.

- To brainstorm a list of common anger triggers in the lives of group members.

Materials needed

- flipchart paper and markers (Chalkboard, dry erase board, or any other visible way to record participant answers will work equally well. Throughout this curriculum, we will use the term "flipchart" for simplicity's sake)

- index cards

- pencils or pens for participants to use to complete written exercises

- (Optional) a folder for each participant, to store group handouts and journal pages from session to session.

Before beginning

- Make "riddle" and "punch line" cards, per the instructions from *The Joker* activity (page 32).

- Pre-print the quote "Do not teach your children never to be angry; teach them how to be angry," by Lyman Abbott, on a flipchart in an easily visible part of the room.

- Prepare copies of the *What is Anger?* handout (page 34) for each participant.

- Prepare copies of the *Weekly journal* (page 36) for each participant.

- Prepare copies of the *Notes for parents* handout (page 37) for each participant to take home.

Welcome to the group

1. Begin with a warm welcome to all participants and a brief introduction to the purpose of the group. In your own words, convey the following:

   - *Everyone feels angry at times. We all make choices every day about how to express that anger.*

   - *This 15-week group experience will help you think about your own anger styles, replace self-defeating patterns, and practice assertive ways to express anger.*

   - *This group is all about self-expression; your participation is highly valued!*

   - *Each group session will revolve around activities, discussions, and group members' real-life experiences.*

2. Introduce yourself, if group participants do not already know you. Tell a bit about your interest in helping kids develop skills for assertive anger expression.

3. If you will have any co-facilitators assisting you with the group, introduce them at this point as well. Tell participants that since they will spend the next 15 sessions sharing their experiences and working together, they'll start this session by getting to know each other better.

Icebreaker activity: The Joker

- The intention of this first group session is to lay the foundation for a trusting, safe atmosphere in which participants can get to know, trust, and help each other.

- Even in groups where kids know each other well, it is important to allow for an "icebreaking" period each session where they can get out of a school/session/treatment mindset and into group mode.

- *The Joker* uses humor to put participants at ease and to build a positive atmosphere for a successful group experience.

- Follow the instructions on *The Joker* activity sheet (page 32) for this five-minute icebreaker.

Group ground rules

Ground rules are critical for helping participants learn what is expected of them in the group setting and also understand how counseling groups function differently than classroom or recreational gatherings (Smead 1995).

- In your own words, explain the importance of establishing group ground rules:
  - *Ground rules are expectations for how we behave in the group and how we treat one another.*
  - *The rules we establish can help us feel safe by letting all of us know the purpose and the limits of the group, including what is expected and what is not permitted.*
- Use flipchart paper and markers to have the group brainstorm ground rules.
- Examples of helpful group ground rules are statements like:
  - *Maintain the confidentiality of what is shared in the group.*
  - *Don't talk while others are talking.*
  - *This is a judgment-free zone! We are here to respect and support each other.*
- In establishing group ground rules, it is most effective to have kids come up with the majority of the rules.
  - Usually, kids generate very good rules. Intervene only if a rule is completely off-base.
  - Intervene by asking other group members what they think about a rule or, in a non-judgmental way, talk about why the rule might not work well in the group.
  - If important rules are omitted by the kids, suggest them at the end of the brainstorming.

Anger Defined

1. Ask for volunteers to offer a definition of "anger."
   - Flipchart key words and phrases, while steering the discussion along the lines of the following definition (Long, Long and Whitson 2009, p.9):
     - Anger is a basic, spontaneous, temporary, internalized feeling, usually triggered by frustration and experienced as an unpleasant state.
     - Anger comes and goes and can be experienced as mild, medium, and intense.

○ While anger is a real, powerful, and natural emotion, it does not always reflect an accurate or objective perception of the triggering event.

2. To illustrate this last point, read the following example aloud (or substitute your own):

Tamara was angry at her mother for making her set the table. She angrily yelled, "You make me do everything around here!" Tamara threw the napkins on the table and stormed out of the room.

3. Summarize the definition of anger by making these points:

○ *We all experience the world differently.*

○ *Some of the things that create powerful feelings of anger in you wouldn't bother your peers in the slightest—and vice versa.*

○ *Then again, there are some things that tend to bother most of us. Next, we'll take a look at some common anger triggers in everyday life.*

Anger Triggers

1. Divide the participants into small groups (3–4 kids per group).

   • Since this is the first group session, it can be helpful for the facilitator to assign kids to specific groups. This eliminates the awkwardness of not knowing where to go or having any participants feel excluded.

   • Fun ways to break kids up into random groups include categories such as:

     ○ kids whose first names begin with a vowel

     ○ kids not wearing socks

     ○ kids over 60 inches (150 cm) tall

     ○ kids who have ever been a ghost for Halloween.

2. Give each participant a copy of the *What is Anger?* handout (pages 34–35), which contains basic definitions of anger, as well as space for the next brainstorming activity.

3. Assign each group to brainstorm one list of common anger triggers (those things in life that would cause most people to feel angry) and one list of personal anger triggers (things that make individual group members angry).

4. Allow about ten minutes for small groups to work together, then reconvene the large group and ask for a representative from each group to report back on the completed lists.

5. Flipchart the responses and provide affirming, supportive statements to group members.

    *   There are no right or wrong answers to this activity.

    *   The responses should provide a good introduction for the participants to understand each other's triggers.

    *   As the kids look over the group list, emphasize that members are not alone in experiencing anger in their lives.

6. This exercise will also help the facilitator gain insight into the common sources of anger among group members. These sources can be drawn upon throughout future sessions, to make the group discussion most relevant to all participants.

7. Direct participants' attention to the Lyman Abbott quotation, pre-printed on flipchart paper.

    *   Ask a volunteer to read the quote aloud to the group.

    *   Ask a different volunteer to explain the meaning of the quote, in their own words.

    *   Emphasize the following:

        ◦   Anger is a natural feeling and that all people have the right to feel angry and to express their anger.

        ◦   Abbott's message is to encourage parents and other adults to teach children How to be angry effectively, or, in other words, to develop skills for assertive anger expression—which is what group members will spend the next 14 group sessions doing.

Session conclusion

1. Summarize the learning from this session and preview next session's agenda:

    *   *Just as adults need to communicate anger effectively in order to succeed in work and relationships, kids can benefit from learning to recognize self-destructive anger expression styles and practicing new, constructive ways to express anger.*

    *   *Next week, we will talk about the four most common anger expression styles: aggression, passivity, passive aggression, and assertiveness.*

2. Hand out the *Weekly journal* page.

3. Let participants know that each week they will have the opportunity to take what they learned in group and apply it to their everyday lives. The weekly journal provides each participant with a chance to reflect on how they are communicating angry feelings, through writing and/or drawing topics.

   - While the weekly journal is an important extension of the group learning, it is not meant to feel like "homework."

   - Use care when describing the journal, to help participants see it as a tool for deeper learning, rather than a burden or obligation.

   - Do not assign penalties for incomplete journals, but rather be consistent in encouraging participants to take this extra step toward replacing self-defeating patterns and committing to new, more effective behaviors.

   - Use discretion in assigning writing journals, art journals, or whatever self-expression method will work best for each participant.

4. Journal topic:

   - This week, write or draw about one thing that created feelings of anger for you and explain what you did to handle your anger.

   - There are no right or wrong answers when it comes to journaling. The purpose of this assignment is to increase awareness of the things that create angry feelings in your daily life and for you to become more aware of which of your responses make a situation worse and which make your life better.

Suggestions for customizing the curriculum

- Younger children or those with less experience working in small groups may have difficulty thinking of helpful or appropriate group ground rules. The facilitator can provide additional help with this activity for participants who need it. Likewise, a facilitator can allow greater independence with this activity for older or more experienced group participants.

- When defining "anger" for participants, use language and terminology that is appropriate for the participants' age and developmental level. Clarify any terms that may be confusing. The point of the activity is to help kids understand that anger is a basic emotion that all people experience, so bringing the term into everyday, accessible language is critical.

- When brainstorming anger triggers, allow participants whose writing skills are not as strong to simply talk about their triggers. Alternately, an adult or designated writer could record answers for group members, rather than assigning each participant to write their own list.

- When describing the weekly journal topics, allow for participants to express themselves in whatever way best helps them to reflect on the subject matter. Some students will enjoy the process of keeping a written journal, others may choose to draw, and still others may opt to talk about the subject matter with a fellow group member or trusted adult over the course of the week.

✓

Icebreaker activity: The Joker

Instructions

1. Prior to the group session, copy the jokes and punch lines from the table below onto index cards.

2. When the session begins, give each participant an index card with either a joke or a punch line. Take care to distribute a corresponding punch line for each joke. If you have an odd number of group participants, an adult facilitator should participate in the activity so that every person is paired at the end of the activity.

3. Instruct participants to find their match—either the joke to their punch line, or the punch line to their joke.

4. Once participants have correctly paired off, instruct them to share basic information about themselves, such as:

   • name

   • age

   • grade (year group)

   • favorite TV show

   • favorite music.

5. Allow about five minutes for the participants to "break the ice" in these dyads, before continuing on.

Processing the activity

• *During the 15 group sessions, there are certain to be many times where someone else will provide a great answer to your question or you will be the one to help solve a problem that has been puzzling someone for years.*

• *We are here to help each other, support each other, and hopefully enjoy some good laughs at the same time!*

Copyright © Signe Whitson 2011

Joke	Punch line
Why did the cookie go to the doctor?	He felt crumb-y
Why should you knock before opening the refrigerator?	Because you might see the salad dressing
What did one volcano say to the other?	"Stop inter-erupt-ing me!"
What time is it when the clock strikes 13?	Time to get a new clock
What did the cat say when it struck out at the baseball game?	Me-out!
What kind of bird never goes to the barber?	A bald eagle
What gets wetter and wetter the more it dries?	A towel
Who goes up but never comes down?	Your age
What kind of dance do teachers like best?	Atten-dance
Where do funny frogs sit?	On silly pads

Copyright © Signe Whitson 2011

✓

Handout: What Is Anger?

- Anger is a real, powerful, natural emotion.

- It is usually triggered by frustration and experienced as an unpleasant feeling.

- Anger comes and goes and can be experienced as mild, medium, and intense (Long *et al.* 2009, p.9).

- Some of the things that create powerful feelings of anger in you wouldn't bother your peer in the slightest—and vice versa.

Common anger triggers:

Copyright © Signe Whitson 2011

Personal anger triggers:

Do not teach your children never to be angry; teach them how to be angry.

Lyman Abbott

We all have the right to feel angry and we also have the right to express our anger. When anger is expressed in assertive ways, our frustration will be reduced and we can improve our relationships.

Copyright © Signe Whitson 2011

Weekly journal

This week, write or draw about something that creates feelings of anger for you. Explain what you did to handle your anger.

There are no right or wrong answers when it comes to journaling. The purpose of this assignment is to increase awareness of the things that create angry feelings in your daily life and for you to become more aware of which of your responses make a situation worse and which make your life better.

Copyright © Signe Whitson 2011

Notes for parents

Often, kids struggle with how to communicate angry feelings. Their emotional pendulum swings between the self-destructive extremes of aggression, passivity, and even passive aggression. The skill-building activities and discussions in this group curriculum help bring the pendulum to rest in a more constructive middle ground, in which kids learn how to express anger effectively, using assertive behaviors to confront and manage real-life situations.

After each session of the *How to Be Angry* group, you will receive a *Notes for parents* handout. These notes offer ideas for real-world discussions and at-home conversation starters, to pick up where group discussions leave off. With messages reinforced both at home and in group, your young person will be in the best position to experience constructive change and develop lasting anger management skills.

Session 1: That Makes Me So Mad! Identifying Common Anger Triggers

- Talk with your child about anger, sharing the highlights of the definition provided in the session and emphasizing that anger is neither good nor bad in and of itself, but rather a normal, powerful emotion that comes and goes in the daily lives of all people.

- Help your child develop a list of the most common triggers for his/her anger. It may be helpful for you to participate along with your child in this activity, creating your own anger triggers list. As the two of you share your lists and compare notes, you gain mutual understanding that can lead to more careful and respectful interactions around "trigger" issues.

- Encourage your child to keep a writing or art journal to record his/her thoughts and feelings about everyday situations that create powerful feelings. There is no need to limit the journal's scope to situations that trigger anger. Rather, keeping a regular journal is a great way for your child to explore and express a range of emotions on a regular basis. As you engage your child in one-on-one discussions that follow the themes of this group curriculum, he/she can use the journal as a place to record new ideas, reflect on self-defeating patterns, and make plans to utilize new, assertive behaviors.

Copyright © Signe Whitson 2011

Session 2

Decisions, Decisions!
Four Choices in Anger Expression

Session objectives

- To define and discuss four anger expression styles.
- To learn specific behaviors characteristic of each anger expression style.
- To identify healthy, constructive ways to express anger.

Materials needed

- pencils or pens for participants to use to complete written exercises
- index cards and tape or Post-it® note paper
- 11 x 14 inch (28 x 35 cm) poster board for anger expression style signs

Before beginning

- Prepare copies of the *Anger Expression Styles* handout (page 44) for each participant.
- Use poster board to post four signs around the group room, one corresponding to each anger expression style (aggressive, passive, passive aggressive and assertive).
- Make anger behavior cards, per the instructions from the *What's Your Style?* activity (page 45).
- Prepare copies of the *Four Choices in Anger Expression* (page 47 or 49) handout for each participant.
- Prepare copies of the *Weekly journal* (page 50) for each participant.
- Prepare copies of the *Notes for parents* handout (page 51) for each participant to take home.

Welcome back

1. Welcome participants back for their second session of the *How to Be Angry* group.

2. Convey that you are eager to get right back into the group interaction and learning about different styles of anger expression.

3. Briefly review group purpose and ground rules.

Icebreaker activity: Journal Sharing, Round Robin Style

1. Arrange the participants in a circle, sitting either on chairs or on the floor. Let kids know that they will be sharing entries from the weekly journals they began after the last session.

2. Ask for a volunteer to begin the sharing. One by one, kids should select one example of something that caused them to feel angry and talk about how they handled their anger.

3. Reassure kids that their example doesn't have to show a "correct" way of handling anger.

    Mistakes are how we learn, so sharing a time when you know you could have responded more effectively will be a helpful learning experience for all.

4. Assure kids that group members will never be forced to share. The more participants open up and share experiences—both the good and the bad— the more everyone will benefit from the group. On the other hand, it is permissible to "pass" on sharing from time to time. Kids should not have to share why they choose to "pass." Allowing kids to make their own decisions about participation builds trust in the group facilitator.

5. Since this activity is meant only as an icebreaker, do not linger too long on any one answer. Affirm each participant's response, thank them for sharing, allow brief comments from group members, and continue until everyone who wants to share has done so.

6. Conclude the icebreaker with an affirmation that anger is a real, powerful, natural emotion that all people experience in their day-to-day lives. The purpose of this group is to explore different anger expression styles and to practice healthy, constructive ways to express anger.

What's Your Style?

1. Give each participant a copy of the *Anger Expression Styles* handout (page 44).

2. Ask for different volunteers to read aloud each of the four definitions of anger expression styles provided on the handout (aggression, passivity, passive aggression, and assertiveness.)

3. Following each definition, verify that participants understand the term that was read aloud by asking for new volunteers to define the anger expression style in their own words. Participants can offer examples of aggressive, passive, passive aggressive, and assertive behaviors to assist with their personal definitions.

4. In your own words, explain why it is important to clarify the definitions:

    *   *The purpose of this group is to learn how to replace the self-defeating patterns of aggression, passivity, and passive aggression with more effective assertive behaviors.*

    *   *Today, we will spend time talking about each style, starting with a game.*

5. Follow the instructions on the *What's Your Style?* activity (page 45) for this five-minute group activity.

6. The *What's Your Style?* activity is designed to help kids learn practical definitions for the four key anger expression styles and begin to identify their own typical style(s).

7. Explain to participants that, through the activities of this group, they will practice skills for assertive self-expression. Emphasize that developing assertiveness will give kids the ability to stand up for what they believe in and get their needs met without violating the rights and needs of others.

The next group activity will review a new scenario and allow kids further practice in differentiating between the four anger expression styles.

Four Choices in Anger Expression scenarios

1. Read (or ask a volunteer to read) the scenario at the top of the chosen *Four Choices in Anger Expression* handout (page 47 or 49).

    Two versions of this handout are included—one about a Nintendo DSi and one revolving around a game of catch. The facilitator may use either or both in the same session.

2. Break the kids into groups of 2–3. Assign groups to discuss each response and identify them as passive, aggressive, passive aggressive, or assertive.

3. Next, kids should rank the responses from most constructive to most destructive, and talk about what might be the result of each response. Allow ten minutes for this discussion.

   The order of the rankings is up to the discussion and discretion of group members. The only firm ranking is the assertive response as the most constructive toward building positive peer relationships.

4. Reconvene the large group, asking each small group to share how they labeled each response, their rankings, and the imagined results of each response.

5. The facilitator should affirm the group responses, making sure to clarify answers and encouraging kids to realize that the assertive response is the one that contributes most constructively to the relationship and to getting the speaker's needs met.

6. Conclude with this emphasis:

   - *We have choices every day in how we respond to a situation.*

   - *We can choose to be passive, aggressive, passive aggressive, or assertive.*

   - *The choices you make elicit predictable responses from others.*

   - *The way you want to be treated by others begins with how you treat them, including how you express your angry thoughts and feelings.*

Session conclusion

1. Summarize the learning from this session and preview next session's agenda:

   - *Kids who learn the skills of assertive self-expression benefit from building positive relationships, standing up for what they believe in, and getting their needs met.*

   - *Next week, we will talk more about the choices we have in the way we express ourselves.*

2. Journal topic:

   - This week, write about a situation (either from the past or during this week) in which someone responds to a situation either passively, aggressively, passive aggressively or assertively. Write about the situation, the response, and why you think the response was effective or not.

- There are no right or wrong answers when it comes to journaling. The purpose of this assignment is to increase awareness about anger expression styles and the choices and consequences of these different responses.

Suggestions for customizing the curriculum

- Younger participants may need additional assistance understanding the language and terminology used to define the four anger expression styles. Be sure to clarify any confusing words and ensure that participants have a solid understanding of the kinds of behaviors that characterize each style.

- In the *What's Your Style?* activity, it may be helpful to use color-coded index cards for each category (e.g. red = aggressive, blue = passive, etc.) to give participants a visual cue for matching a behavior with the correct anger expression style. The colored cards can also be made to correspond to a colored poster board, featuring each anger expression style.

- Two versions of the *Four Choices in Anger Expression* handout are provided. The facilitator may choose to use one or both, depending on the size, needs, and interests of group members. Younger participants or those with more difficulty reading independently may do better working on this activity as a large group, rather than in small groups.

✓

Handout: Anger Expression Styles

Aggression

Aggression is one way the feeling of anger is expressed in behavior. Aggression is usually impulsive and unplanned. Aggressive behavior is destructive to relationships because it aims to hurt or damage a person or an object. Aggression can be physical (e.g. punching, kicking) or verbal (e.g. threatening, calling names).

Passivity

Passive people express needs, wants and feelings in an indirect way. They feel that their needs are not as important as the needs of others, so they behave in ways that allow their needs to be ignored or overlooked. Passive behaviors may take the form of poor eye contact or soft speech.

Passive aggressive

Passive aggressive behavior is a hidden way of expressing feelings of anger. It involves behaviors designed to get back at another person without the person recognizing the hidden anger. Passive aggressive behaviors include procrastinating, carrying out chores or tasks the wrong way, sulking, or getting hidden revenge.

Assertiveness

Assertiveness is a style that is used to express anger in words, in a direct and respectful way. Assertive behavior sets limits on what a person is willing or not willing to do in a situation. It is an honest form of communication in which a person expresses their wants and needs without hurting or violating the rights of others. Assertiveness includes behaviors like good eye contact, even tone of voice, and the use of I-Messages.

Note: Definitions of aggression, passivity, passive aggression and assertiveness are adapted from *The Angry Smile: The Psychology of Passive-Aggressive Behavior in Families, Schools, and Workplaces*, 2nd edn (pp.9–12), by J.E. Long, N.J. Long and S. Whitson, 2009, Austin, TX: PRO-ED. Copyright 2009 by PRO-ED, Inc. Adapted with permission.

Copyright © Signe Whitson 2011

Activity: What's Your Style?

For the facilitator

1. Before the group session begins, print one aggressive, passive, passive aggressive or assertive behavior (listed below) on each index card.

2. Create enough cards so that each group participant receives 1–2 behavioral examples.

3. Tell participants to read the behavior on their card and match it to the correct anger expression style sign, posted around the room.

    - Provide tape for participants to affix their card to the wall, under the proper sign.

    - Post-it® note paper also works well, as a substitute for index cards, for this activity.

    - If a participant is unsure of how to categorize the behavior on his card, he can ask for help from the facilitator or a peer.

4. Once the participants have posted all of their cards (under five minutes), review the activity as a group.

    - Ask for volunteers to read aloud the cards under each anger expression style.

    - Ask the larger group to confirm agreement or disagreement with the way the cards are categorized.

    - If an incorrect answer is identified, ask participants to determine its correct categorization and explain the rationale behind the correct answer.

    - Ask participants to consider if there is one particular style that they tend to rely upon to express anger and to begin thinking about how this style impacts their relationships.

Copyright © Signe Whitson 2011

✔

Aggressive behaviors:	Passive behaviors:
• shoving • punching • cursing • calling names • interrupting.	• not expressing an opinion, even when asked • pretending not to care • avoiding eye contact • speaking in a soft voice • running away.
Passive aggressive behaviors:	Assertive behaviors:
• sulking • procrastinating • pretending to forget to do an important chore • getting revenge in a secret way • purposely doing a poor job on a chore or assignment.	• looking someone in the eye when speaking • using I-Messages to express feelings • using a calm, even tone of voice • speaking at a regular volume • expressing your needs without disrespecting others.

Copyright © Signe Whitson 2011

Handout: Four Choices in Anger Expression (1)

Mel's class earned the privilege to bring a game to school on Friday and use it during a special free period. Mel looked forward to Friday all week. When the afternoon free period finally arrived, she was excited to try out a brand new game on her Nintendo DSi.

Just as she was taking the DSi from the case, her friend Nikki came up behind her, grabbed the case, and picked out a game cartridge. "Can I play this one?" she asked. Before Mel could answer, Richie walked over and claimed, "I get to play after Nikki!"

Mel looked up to see a line forming behind Richie and Nikki and heard everyone asking for a turn to play her Nintendo. The noise was making her frustrated and she was getting angry about wasting the free period without getting any of her own play time.

1. Match each of Mel's possible responses to the correct anger expression style (passive, aggressive, passive aggressive or assertive).

2. Rate each response on a scale of 1–4, from most constructive (1) to most destructive (4), when it comes to Mel forming positive peer relationships.

3. Imagine how Mel's peers would react to each of her possible responses.

Copyright © Signe Whitson 2011

Mel's response	Anger expression style	Ranking (1–4)	Probable peer reactions
Mel rips the case back out of Nikki's hands and storms away, yelling "Get your own Nintendo and leave my stuff alone!"	Aggressive		
Mel sits quietly while each peer takes a turn playing with her DSi. She allows others to play for the entire free period and misses her own turn.	Passive		
Mel explains to her peers that she has been looking forward to trying out a new game all week and would be happy to let everyone take a turn, as long as she gets the chance to first play her game.	Assertive		
Mel secretly disables the DSi before handing it to Nikki, then lets Nikki take the heat from everyone for breaking the game and ruining their chance to play.	Passive aggressive		

Copyright © Signe Whitson 2011

Handout: Four Choices in Anger Expression (2)

Ty brings his football outside during school recess. He invites a group of kids to play. His peers agree right away and quickly organize teams. When play begins, Ty soon realizes that he is being excluded from his own game. No one is throwing him the ball or including him in any of the plays. He is feeling humiliated and angry.

1. Match each of Ty's possible responses to the correct anger expression style (passive, aggressive, passive aggressive or assertive).

2. Rate each response on a scale of 1–4, from most constructive (1) to most destructive (4), when it comes to Ty forming positive peer relationships.

3. Imagine how Ty's peers would react to each of his possible responses.

Ty's response	Anger expression style	Ranking (1–4)	Probable peer reactions
Ty tries to catch up to his teammates as they discuss strategy and does his best to keep up with the action, despite being left out of what is going on.	Passive		
At the next time out, Ty explains to his peers that he brought the football so that he could play and he would be happy to continue sharing the ball as long as he is included in game plans and plays.	Assertive		
Ty gets the ball during a time out and throws it as hard as he can at a peer, hitting him in the stomach. When the peer asks, "What did you do that for?" Ty innocently shrugs and says, "Oh—sorry. I thought you were expecting it."	Passive aggressive		
Ty grabs the ball from a teammate, shoves him to the ground, and yells, "Next time, I'm calling the plays!"	Aggressive		

Copyright © Signe Whitson 2011

Weekly journal

This week, write or draw about a situation (either from the past or during this week) in which someone responds to a situation either passively, aggressively, passive aggressively or assertively. Describe the situation, the response, and why you think the response was effective or not.

There are no right or wrong answers when it comes to journaling. The purpose of this assignment is to increase awareness about anger expression styles and the choices and consequences of these different responses.

Copyright © Signe Whitson 2011

Notes for parents from Session 2

Decisions, Decisions! Four Choices in Anger Expression

- Talk with your child about the four anger expression styles discussed in the group. Invite him/her to define each style in his/her own terms, using specific behaviors or real-life examples to clarify its meaning. Share your own perspective on each style, describing varied situations in which you have behaved in each way.

- When you encounter situations in your daily life, or while watching TV or browsing online, identify the real-world behaviors that characterize aggressive, passive, passive aggressive and assertive styles. Challenge your child to recognize these behaviors in real life and to talk about which behaviors appear to strengthen a relationship vs. which ones are damaging to relationships.

- Use the *Four Choices in Anger Expression* handout with your child to spark discussion about destructive vs. constructive anger expression styles.

Copyright © Signe Whitson 2011

Sugarcoated Hostility
The Five Levels of Passive Aggressive Behavior

Session objectives

- To further define passive aggressive behavior as a self-defeating anger expression style.
- To learn five distinct levels of passive aggressive behavior.
- To identify personal behaviors that are passive aggressive.

Materials needed

- 11 x 14 inch (28 x 35 cm) poster board for *Do I Do This?* activity signs

Before beginning

- Prepare copies of *The Five Levels of Passive Aggressive Behavior* handout (page 58) for each participant.
- Use poster board to post three signs around the group room (Most of the time, Some of the time, None of the time) for the *Do I Do This?* activity (page 60).
- Prepare copies of the *Weekly journal* (page 64) for each participant.
- Prepare copies of the *Notes for parents* handout (page 65) for each participant to take home.

Welcome back

1. Welcome participants to the third group session.

2. Let participants know that they are not going to share journal entries specifically this session, but ask if any member wants to share an interesting experience or observation about anger styles or expression that occurred since the last session.

Icebreaker activity: Name That Style

1. *Last week, we talked about four anger expression styles.* Ask these questions as a quick review:

   * *Who can name all four styles?* (passive, aggressive, passive aggressive and assertive)

   * *Who can give a quick definition of each?* (ask for one volunteer for each term)

   * *Which anger expression style is the most constructive for building positive relationships?* (assertiveness)

2. *Before we begin our main activity today, we are going to play a quick group game about constructive (assertive) and destructive (aggressive, passive, passive aggressive) anger expression styles.*

   * Divide the participants into four separate groups. Without the other groups hearing, assign each small group one of the four anger expression styles.

   * Assign each group to create a two-minute play that shows a person communicating anger according to the assigned style.

   * Groups should perform their plays for the large group and allow their audience the chance to correctly identify the anger expression style they are portraying.

   * Debrief the activity, encouraging kids to share their answers and thoughts.

The Five Levels of Passive Aggressive Behavior

1. Review the definition of "anger" discussed in the first group session:

   - Anger is a real, powerful, and natural emotion usually triggered by frustration and experienced as an unpleasant state.

   - Anger comes and goes and can be experienced as mild, medium, and intense (Long *et al.* 2009, p.9).

2. Preview this week's objective:

   We have spent time brainstorming common anger triggers in our lives and talked about the four basic styles of anger expression. Today, we will be focusing on the passive aggressive style of anger expression.

3. Carefully review these definitions of passive aggression (included in *The Five Levels of Passive Aggressive Behavior* handout (page 58)).

   Passive aggression:

   - is a deliberate and masked way of expressing hidden feelings of anger (Long *et al.* 2009, pp.12–13)

   - involves a variety of behaviors designed to get back at another person without the person recognizing the underlying anger

   - is often even more destructive to relationships than aggression, since the indirectness of the anger expression creates mistrust, confusion, dishonesty, and frustration

   - is motivated by a person's fear of expressing anger directly.

   Examples of common passive aggressive behaviors include:

   - procrastinating

   - giving someone the silent treatment

   - sulking

   - carrying out chores or responsibilities in an inefficient way

   - getting secret revenge

   - "forgetting" to give someone an important message.

4. Tell participants that passive aggressive behavior generally occurs on five distinct levels. Explain:

- *We are going to do an activity to identify each level.*

- *When we are aware of our own passive aggressive behaviors at the various levels, we are best able to stop them and replace them with more assertive, direct communication.*

5. Direct participants to note the three poster board signs hung around the room and let them know they will be walking back and forth between the signs to show their agreement with each of the situations described in the upcoming activity.

6. Read aloud each passive aggressive scenario from the *Do I Do This?* activity (page 60).

    - Participants are to walk to one assigned end of the room if they know that they respond that way *most* of the time.

    - Participants are to walk a different assigned end of the room if they know that they respond that way *some* of the time.

    - Participants are to walk to a third assigned end of the room if they know that they respond that way *none* of the time.

7. After the participants have arranged themselves around the room under the proper poster, the facilitator should further define each level of passive aggressive behavior, according to the definitions provided on the activity sheet.

This learning activity is designed to inspire insight and understanding as participants move around the room, learning about each other's typical responses, and gaining new knowledge of the five distinct levels of passive aggressive behavior.

- Participants often experience "A-ha!" moments when they realize that the way they respond "most" or "some" of the time is a type of passive aggression. With this knowledge, they can begin to change this self-defeating behavior pattern.

- During this activity, some participants may feel embarrassed or ashamed to admit that they use passive aggressive behaviors. Reassure all participants that:

  ○ *most people use passive aggressive behaviors from time to time*

  ○ *standing under a particular poster need not be something to be embarrassed about*

  ○ *your participation in the activity is a sign of strength that you are willing to learn about and acknowledge a self-defeating anger expression pattern*

  ○ *the only way to change self-defeating patterns is to first understand and "own" them.*

- Participants should be invited to share examples of times that they have seen others behave in passive aggressive ways that match the descriptions of each level.

- The facilitator's role is to guide the discussion and encourage insight. The facilitator should be very familiar with the five levels of passive aggressive behavior and should be able to ask questions of the participants that encourage learning, discussion and self-reflection.

Session conclusion

1. Summarize the learning from this session and preview next week's agenda:

   - *This week, we focused the five levels of passive aggressive behavior.*

   - *Next week, we will do a creative activity that helps us consider the ways we present ourselves to others.*

2. Journal topic:

   - If you encounter any examples of passive aggressive behavior this week, make a note of them in your journal. Describe the situation and try to identify the correct level of passive aggression that the behavior fits into.

   - The purpose of this assignment is to create daily awareness of passive aggressive behavior and to understand how it causes long-term damage to relationships.

Suggestions for customizing the curriculum

- Younger participants may need additional assistance understanding the language and terminology used to define passive aggressive behavior. Use specific behavioral examples and common, real-world scenarios to help participants gain a clear understanding of passive aggression as a self-defeating pattern of behavior. Encourage participants to take the handout with them after group and to discuss it with an adult, who can assist them with any of the difficult language.

- The scenarios in the *Do I Do This?* activity can be customized according to the ages, abilities, and issues relevant to group members. Prior to the group session, the facilitator can develop new scenarios, or tweak the ones provided, to optimize the learning for each group.

Handout: The Five Levels of Passive Aggressive Behavior

Passive aggression is an intentional, but hidden, way of expressing anger. It involves a variety of behaviors designed to get back at another person without the person recognizing the underlying anger. Passive aggressive behavior creates mistrust, confusion, and frustration.

Passive aggressive behavior occurs on five distinct levels:

Level 1: Temporary compliance

Temporary compliance occurs when a person agrees to a request, but then doesn't actually carry it out. For example, a kid might say, "I'm coming" when his father asks him to turn off the TV and start mowing the lawn, but then never actually get around to carrying out the chore. When his father asks about it later in the day, the kid might pretend, "Oh, sorry. I forgot."

Level 2: Intentional inefficiency

Intentional inefficiency occurs when a person carries out a request in a purposefully unacceptable way. For example, a child might complete all of the answers from his social studies homework, but in such messy handwriting that his teacher cannot understand what he wrote.

Level 3: Letting a problem escalate

Letting a problem escalate is a way of expressing anger toward another person by choosing not to share some knowledge when it would prevent a problem. For example, a kid might notice that a piece of paper has fallen out of a classmate's backpack, but rather than alert her, he lets her walk away. He sees that she has lost her book report, but takes no action to try to return it to her, knowing that the girl will have a serious problem in her next class.

Copyright © Signe Whitson 2011

Level 4: Hidden but conscious revenge

Hidden but conscious revenge occurs when a person makes a deliberate decision to get back at someone else by secretly damaging his reputation, frustrating his daily activities, or damaging and stealing objects of importance. For example, a kid uses MySpace to spread a cruel rumor about a teacher that he dislikes.

Level 5: Self-depreciation

Self-depreciation is the most serious level of passive aggression. It occurs when a person is so angry and fixated at getting back at someone else that he is willing to allow himself to be hurt in the process. For example, a student refuses to do his homework or study because he knows how much his bad grades will bother his mother.

Note: Titles and definitions of the "five levels of passive aggressive behavior" are adapted from *The Angry Smile: The Psychology of Passive-Aggressive Behavior in Families, Schools, and Workplaces*, 2nd edn (pp.41–56), by J.E. Long, N.J. Long and S. Whitson, 2009, Austin, TX: PRO-ED. Copyright 2009 by PRO-ED, Inc. Adapted with permission.

Activity: Do I Do This? The Five Levels of Passive Aggressive Behavior

Level 1: Temporary compliance

Your teacher tells you to put away a book you are reading and begin your math workbook. You know that math isn't supposed to begin for another five minutes and you're angry that she's cutting short your free time. Plus, you only have three more pages in the chapter and you really want to know what happens before you close the book.

The first time she tells you, you pretend you don't hear her.

The second time she tells you, you answer, "OK, I'll start math in just a second," but never look up from your book.

The third time, she loses her cool in front of the whole class. You close your book calmly, look at her with a little smile on your face, and say, "I don't know what you're getting so upset about. I'm opening my book right now. I thought teachers were supposed to be able to hold it together better."

Your teacher is clearly embarrassed at her overreaction. You feel satisfied with how things have turned out.

For the facilitator

After participants have chosen where to stand in the room and discussed their choices, offer this definition of *temporary compliance*:

- Temporary compliance occurs when a person verbally agrees to do something, but behaviorally delays.

- This is the most common form of passive aggressive behavior.

- Temporary compliance typically involves procrastinating over a task or pretending not to hear a request, see a particular object, or remember to do something.

- Temporary compliance is a way of acting out the anger about a original request (e.g. "Put away your book and start math") in a hidden way and taking pleasure in getting the requestor to act out the anger instead.

- Temporary compliance is an indirect way of communicating anger and one that is destructive to relationships in the long term.

Copyright © Signe Whitson 2011

Level 2: Intentional inefficiency

Your dad tells you to pack nice clothes for a weekend trip to your grandmother's house. You will be gathering with 20 family members at a fine dining restaurant to celebrate your grandmother's 75th birthday. Your grandmother has never even been all that nice to you and you are sick of your dad criticizing what you wear and wanting you to dress in preppy clothes.

You do as you are told, packing a button-down shirt and the tie your father bought you for your birthday. When it's time to dress for the birthday dinner, you appear in the wrinkled shirt, stained tie, and a pair of ripped khakis. Your father hits the roof when he sees you, frightening your grandmother.

You calmly shrug your shoulders and say, "I don't know why you're so upset. I packed exactly what you asked me to. Your problem is that you want everything to be done your way—perfectly!"

For the facilitator

After participants have chosen where to stand in the room and discussed their choices, offer this definition of *intentional inefficiency*:

- Intentional inefficiency occurs when a person complies with a given request but carries it out in an unacceptable way.

- Often, the person who made the request is so upset by the level of performance that he ends up doing the task (e.g. father will pack the clothes next time) or does not make the request again in the future (kid can wear whatever he wants).

- By using intentional inefficiency, a person loses by winning. While he gains temporary emotional satisfaction out of getting another person to act out their anger, he damages relationships and frustrates those who could be his important supports and allies.

Level 3: Letting a problem escalate

While getting ready for school in the morning, you hear a news story on the radio of a major traffic accident on the interstate that has resulted in a six-mile backup. You know this is the route your mother will be traveling to the airport, but you choose not to tell her about what you know because you are still angry with her over the argument you had last night. You figure that missing her plane is about what she deserves. Not sharing what you know is a perfect way to get back at her.

Copyright © Signe Whitson 2011

For the facilitator

After participants have chosen where to stand in the room and discussed their choices, offer this definition of *letting a problem escalate*:

- Letting a problem escalate is a more serious and deliberate way of expressing personal anger toward another person by choosing not to share some knowledge when it would prevent a problem.

- The person realizes that by not acting on his knowledge or observation, the person he is angry at will have a serious problem.

- Letting a problem escalate is a guilt-free expression of anger. The person can honestly say he didn't *do* anything. It is by *not doing* something that he caused a problem and acted out his anger.

Level 4: Hidden but conscious revenge

You are mad at your former best friend, Brandi, for ditching you. The two of you had been best friends since fourth grade (9–10 years old), but now that she has a boyfriend and hangs out with his football team friends, she acts like she's too good for you.

You anonymously post embarrassing pictures of her online and secretly spread vicious rumors about her. The whole school is talking about her and she is completely humiliated. You think she deserves to feel this way for a while.

For the facilitator

After participants have chosen where to stand in the room and discussed their choices, offer this definition of *hidden but conscious revenge*:

- Hidden but conscious revenge occurs when a person makes a deliberate decision to get back at someone else by damaging their reputation, frustrating their daily activities, or damaging and stealing objects of importance.

- All of these hostile acts are achieved without the person's knowledge.

- The passive aggressive person feels he has been mistreated, so he feels justified in taking his revenge.

- Other hidden but conscious revenge behaviors include:
  ◦ hiding a teacher's keys
  ◦ stealing money from a parent's wallet
  ◦ destroying a classmate's school project right before it is due.

Copyright © Signe Whitson 2011

Level 5: Self-depreciation

You feel like your mother tries to control you. She is always telling you what to eat, what to wear, who to hang out with, how to do your hair, and what you should be when you grow up. She doesn't want you to date and calls any friend you bring home a "bad influence."

The minute you have a chance to rebel, you do. Over her objections, you start to date a guy who is eight years older than you. He is nice most of the time, but has a bad temper and is really mean to you when he is mad. You know you should break up with him, but choose not to because as badly as he can make you feel, he bothers your mother ten times as much!

For the facilitator

After participants have chosen where to stand in the room and discussed their choices, offer this definition of *self-depreciation*:

- Self-depreciation is the most serious level of passive aggression. It occurs when a person is so angry and fixated on getting back at someone else that he is willing to allow himself to be hurt in the process.

- The person engages in self-destructive behaviors just to get back at someone else.

- In this most serious form of passive aggressive communication, the person is willing to cause damage to his own life in dramatic and lasting ways in order to bring pain and suffering to the person he is angry at.

Copyright © Signe Whitson 2011

Weekly journal

This week, write or draw about any passive aggressive behaviors you observe or encounter. Try to identify the correct level of passive aggression that the behavior fits into.

The purpose of this assignment is to create daily awareness of passive aggressive behavior and to understand how it causes long-term damage to relationships.

Copyright © Signe Whitson 2011

Notes for parents from Session 3

Sugarcoated Hostility: The Five Levels of Passive Aggressive Behavior

- Talk with your child about passive aggressive behavior, elaborating on the definition that was shared when discussing four anger expression styles.

- Use *The Five Levels of Passive Aggressive Behavior* handout to share with your child the different types of passive aggressive behavior and ask for his/her thoughts about passive aggression. Encourage your child to talk about different real-life examples of this behavior.

- If passive aggressive behavior is a troublesome pattern in your family, open a dialogue with your child about family members working together to develop skills to communicate anger more assertively. Focus on the benefits each family member can experience by replacing self-defeating passive aggression with assertiveness, including more honest and less hostile relationships with one another.

- For further reading on the subject of passive aggression, check out *The Angry Smile: The Psychology of Passive Aggressive Behavior in Families, Schools, and Workplaces*, 2nd edn (Long *et al.* 2009). *The Angry Smile* provides step-by-step guidance for parents and professionals in how to stop frustrating arguments, endless conflict cycles, and relationship-damaging wars of words, by using the skill of *benign confrontation*.

Copyright © Signe Whitson 2011

Behind the Mask
Exploring Public Faces and Private Realities

Session objectives

- To develop insight into the differences between private realities and public faces.

- To identify how assertive behaviors help kids express their inner thoughts and feelings.

Materials needed

- colorful candies (enough for each participant to get three pieces) or a set of dice

- simple mask making materials, including:
  - paper plates
  - colored markers and/or pencils
  - construction paper
  - scissors
  - glue
  - other embellishments, as desired and available.

Before beginning

- Set the mask making materials on various tables or work stations around the room.

- Prepare copies of the *Weekly journal* (page 71) for each participant.
- Prepare copies of the *Notes for parents* handout (page 72) for each participant to take home.

Welcome back

1. Welcome participants back for the fourth group session.

2. Remind participants of all that has been learned thus far: common anger triggers, four anger expression styles, and five levels of passive aggressive behavior.

3. Tell participants that the learning will continue today with a fun and creative activity that encourages group members to think about the differences between their inner worlds of thoughts and feelings and the behaviors that they show to the outside world.

Icebreaker activity: Pick a Mix

1. This activity can be done with any colorful candy or sweets, such as M&Ms®, Skittles®, Smarties® or jellybeans. Alternately, dice can be used.

2. Participants should sit together in a circle. If candies or sweets are to be used:

    - The facilitator should offer each person the chance to choose any three pieces of candy, in any combination of colors. Participants should not eat the candy (yet) but rather keep the candy in their hands.

    - After everyone has made their selection, the facilitator should tell participants that they are each going to share three interesting facts about themselves, based on the color of candy in their hand. For example:

        ◦ red candy = your favorite Hollywood star

        ◦ blue candy = a hobby or sport you enjoy

        ◦ green candy = what you want to be when you grow up

        ◦ yellow candy = your age

        ◦ orange candy = your favorite kind of music/musical group

        ◦ purple candy = favorite book, movie, or video game

- ○ Colors and topics can be changed as necessary, but aim for "low-risk," fun items that most people would be readily willing to share.

- ○ If dice are used, simply pass one die around for each participant to roll and assign the topics based on the number each person rolls.

- The facilitator should go first to model the activity, then select the person to his left to speak. Continue all the way around the circle.

The purpose of the activity is to get participants talking and beginning to share low-risk information about their personal lives, as a lead-in to this group session's agenda.

Mask Making

1. Explain that often people create "masks" to hide their true feelings. Over time, this "mask" becomes the face they show to the world across most situations.

2. Using the template in the handout or other simple mask-making materials (paper plates, markers, glue, colored paper, etc.), participants are invited to:

   - first, design a mask that represents which anger expression style they most often show to the outside world

   - then, on the inside of the mask, show how they really feel most of the time.

   Allow at least 20 minutes for this activity, reminding kids about halfway through to work on both sides of the mask. Let them know they will be encouraged to share their mask with the group.

3. Reconvene participants and ask for volunteers to share their masks and discuss the differences between the side they tend to show to the world and the inside that represents how they genuinely feel. Encourage group discussion about the following:

   - *All of us have a private reality that differs from what we show to the public world.*

   - *For some (i.e. the passive aggressive youth) the gap between these two is so large that it interferes with their ability to express thoughts and feelings with authenticity.*

   - *This difficulty with honest and direct expression makes it more difficult to develop close, trusting relationships.*

Note: The idea for the Mask Making activity was originally developed by Jodi Campbell. Adapted with permission.

4. Remind group members that one of the main purposes of the group is to teach them about choices in expressing anger and that upcoming sessions will focus on practicing constructive, safe ways to show their real, authentic feelings to the world.

Session conclusion

1. *Kids benefit from gaining self-understanding about the co-existence of their private reality and their public mask. Relationships improve and trust increases when kids learn constructive, safe ways to express their true feelings and close the gap between their private and public faces.*

2. *Next week, we will talk about the incredibly powerful ways in which body language and tone of voice express thoughts and feelings.*

3. Journal topic:

   - Write about a person with whom you feel safe to communicate your genuine, inner feelings. Who is this person? What is it about this person that allows you to trust him/her and feel safe to express yourself honestly?

   - There are no right or wrong answers when it comes to journaling. The purpose of this assignment is to increase awareness about the qualities to look for in good friends and supportive adults.

Suggestions for customizing the curriculum

The mask-making activity has been used with participants ranging in age from elementary school children to high school and college students and even adults attending professional training workshops. Though on first glance, the creative activity may seem child-like, the message behind the artwork is profound for participants across the age span. Older students may be able to process the discussion about differences between private realities and public behaviors at a deeper level than younger ones; follow-up questions should be tailored according to participant ages and abilities.

Weekly journal

Write or draw about a person with whom you feel safe to communicate your genuine, inner feelings. Who is this person? What is it about this person that allows you to trust him/her and feel safe to express yourself honestly?

There are no right or wrong answers when it comes to journaling. The purpose of this assignment is to increase awareness about the qualities to look for in good friends and supportive adults.

Copyright © Signe Whitson 2011

✓

Notes for parents from Session 4

Behind the Mask: Exploring Public Faces and Private Realities

- During the group session, kids created double-sided masks. The outside of the mask was designed to represent the public face that your child shows to the world. The inside of the mask represents his/her private reality—his/her most genuine thoughts and feelings. Group members shared their masks with one another and talked about the fact that although all of us have a private reality that differs from what we show to the public world, when the gap between realities is too large, the ability to express thoughts and feelings authentically is compromised. Skills for assertive self-expression are useful in closing the gap between public faces and private realities.

- Invite your child to share his/her mask with you. Ask him/her to describe it, as the kids did in the group setting. Refrain from asking too many questions; simply listen and see what you can learn from your child's self-reflection.

- This activity can be replicated at home. Even if your child has already created a mask in group, he/she may be drawn to the task again, as a pairs activity. Work alongside your child, creating your own mask and sharing equally in the experience of reflecting on the difference between private realities and public behaviors. Children will be more willing to create and share authentically when they believe that the process will be a mutual one.

Copyright © Signe Whitson 2011

More than Words Can Express

How Body Language and Tone of Voice Can Say It All

Session objectives

- To learn how powerful the body can be in communicating meaning, even in the absence of words.
- To understand how tone of voice impacts the meaning of words.
- To identify assertive non-verbal behaviors.

Materials needed

- index cards for the *More than Words Can Express* activity.

Before beginning

- Make "task" and "feelings" cards, per the instructions from the *More than Words Can Express* activity (page 78).
- Prepare copies of the *It's not the Words You Use but the Tone You Choose* handout (page 80) for each participant.
- Prepare copies of the *Weekly journal* (page 81) for each participant.
- Prepare copies of the *Notes for parents* handout (page 82) for each participant to take home.

Welcome back

1. Welcome participants back to the fifth session of the group.

2. Preview the agenda for this session:

    - *Last week, we created masks to represent our inner thoughts and feelings.*

    - *Today, we will be doing two fun activities to learn about how important our bodies and our voice are in communicating those thoughts and feelings to others.*

Icebreaker activity: Birthday Order

1. Challenge participants to arrange themselves in a line at the front of the room in order of the month and day of their birth. From left to right, across the room, kids should stand in order of the month of the year when they were born (January–December). Explain to participants that they are not arranging themselves by age, but simply by time of year.

2. The object is to communicate their birth dates to each other *without talking!*

3. Give participants several minutes to figure out how to communicate their birth month and dates non-verbally and to arrange themselves in a line.

4. When they are done, have the kids say their birth date aloud and verify that they are in the correct order.

5. Encourage participants to have fun with this activity. If kids realize they are in the wrong order, they should simply switch and find humor in the challenge of the game.

6. Explain:

    - *The purpose of this icebreaker is to get you thinking about non-verbal communication.*

    - *Today, we will be focusing on how we express emotion using body language and tone of voice.*

More than Words Can Express

More than Words Can Express is a game designed to teach kids how powerful their bodies can be in communicating meaning, even in the absence of words.

Just as the participants communicated about their birth dates without saying a word, they can express a great deal of meaning to others without ever opening their mouths.

1. In this exercise, participants will be given a certain task (e.g. sweeping the floor) to act out at the front of the room. Everyone will know the task, but only the volunteer will be given a card with a feeling word. The volunteer is to act out the given task according to the assigned feeling. Audience members will try to guess the emotion by studying the volunteer's body language.

   • "Task" and "feeling" card ideas are in the *More than Words Can Express* activity sheet (page 78).

   • Allow at least 4–5 volunteers to have a turn acting out their feelings.

   • For discussion:

     ○ *What were some of the key things the volunteers did to show their emotions without speaking?*

     ○ *How do facial expressions convey emotion?* (encourage participants to give specifics about eye contact, staring, glaring, not looking, tensed foreheads, frowns, smiles, raised eyebrows, throat clearing, etc.)

     ○ *How can we use our eyes to communicate assertively?* (maintaining eye contact, etc.)

     ○ *How does posture convey emotion?* (encourage participants to give specifics about crossed arms, standing too close, standing too far, pacing, touching jewelry, looking at watch, etc.)

     ○ *To communicate assertively, what kind of distance should you maintain from your listener?* (not in their face, not too far apart)

It's not the Words You Use but the Tone You Choose

1. Tell participants:

   Along with facial expressions and posture, a third important way that people communicate with their bodies is through their tone of voice. Very often, the words you choose are less important than the tone of voice that you use.

2. Organize participants into pairs or groups of three. Using the *It's not the Words You Use but the Tone You Choose* handout (page 80), participants should take turns saying each sentence.

3. To tie this in with previous group material, participants should alternate saying the sentence using aggressive, passive, and assertive anger expression styles.

4. Ask participants to listen closely to one another and note how the same sentence sounds completely different and sends a distinct message, depending on the tone of voice and anger expression style used.

5. Encourage participants to add in gestures and facial expressions to support their tone of voice.

6. For discussion:

   • *How did changing your tone of voice change the meaning of the sentence?*

   • *What kind of tone of voice conveys an assertive message?* (even voice, neutral tone, not shouting, not whispering, not mumbling, etc.)

7. Emphasize that body language and tone of voice are far more important than words in communicating our true feelings:

   • *When learning to communicate assertively, it is critical that we use our bodies and our voices to support our assertive words.*

Session conclusion

1. *This week, we focused on how we express emotions through our body language and tone of voice.*

2. *Next week, we will be focusing on using assertive wording when we speak, by practicing the skill of creating I-Messages.*

3. Journal topic:

   Take particular notice this week of how those around you use their body language, facial expressions, and tone of voice to communicate emotions. What are some of the things you see people doing? Write them down in your journal, along with a record of how you find yourself using body language and tone of voice to express emotion.

Suggestions for customizing the curriculum

- Younger children may benefit from hints and suggestions from the facilitator on how to act out various "tasks" and "feelings" in the *More than Words Can Express* activity. If group members have a difficult time guessing the correct feeling that is being acted out, the facilitator can provide extra clues and hints. Likewise, the facilitator can choose to limit the Feeling cards used with younger participants to the basic emotions of sad, mad, happy and scared.

- For older participants, facilitators can choose to increase the level of sophistication of the feeling words used and/or the tasks being acted out. The facilitator can also challenge the participants to guess the correct feeling within a certain time frame (e.g. one minute or less).

- If younger participants have difficulty reading the sentences or choosing an accurate tone of voice in the *It's not the Words You Use but the Tone You Choose* activity, the facilitator can role model the first few examples and offer suggestions as the small groups work practice the skill. Alternately, this activity can be done as a large group so that the facilitator can offer greater role-modeling and assistance to all participants.

- To increase the level of challenge in this activity, have older participants create their own sentences and practice saying them according to the four anger expression styles.

Activity: More than Words Can Express

- In this exercise, each participant should be given one card pre-printed with a *task* (e.g. sweeping the floor) and one separate card with a *feeling* (e.g. angry).

- Taking turns, each participant is given the opportunity to act out the given task according to the assigned emotion.

- All group members can know the assigned task, but participants should keep the feeling card private.

- Group members will try to guess the feeling that is being acted out by studying the volunteer's body language.

- The facilitator can mix and match the tasks and feelings cards, and also add additional ones.

Copyright © Signe Whitson 2011

Tasks and feelings cards

Task	Feeling
Sweeping the floor	Angry
Making a phone call	Sad
Putting on shoes	Scared
Straightening up the furniture in a room	Happy
Putting on a coat	Frustrated
Reading a book	Bored
Listening to music	Surprised
Brushing hair	Confused
Writing on a piece of paper	Tired
Eating a sandwich	Excited

Copyright © Signe Whitson 2011

✓

Handout: It's not the Words You Use but the Tone You Choose

- Take turns saying each sentence, using different anger expression styles (passive, aggressive, and assertive).

- Listen closely to one another and note how the same sentence sounds completely different and sends a distinct message, depending on the tone of voice and anger expression style used.

- Add in gestures and facial expressions to support your tone of voice.

1. I was sitting there.

2. Thank you.

3. I want you to ask before you borrow my things.

4. You ate the last piece of pizza.

5. You play with different rules than I do.

6. Pass the peanut butter.

7. You got a new outfit.

8. Is it time to go yet?

9. What is your name?

10. I'm sorry.

Remember: Body language and tone of voice are far more important than words in communicating our true feelings. *When learning to communicate assertively, it is critical that we use our bodies and our voices to support our assertive words.*

Copyright © Signe Whitson 2011

Weekly journal

Take notice this week of how those around you use their body language, facial expressions, and tone of voice to communicate emotions. What are some of the things you see people doing? Write or draw about them in your journal, along with a record of how you find yourself using body language and tone of voice to express emotion.

There are no right or wrong answers when it comes to journaling. The purpose of this assignment is to increase awareness about how body language and tone of voice are used to convey emotion.

Copyright © Signe Whitson 2011

Notes for parents from Session 5

More than Words Can Express: How Body Language and Tone of Voice Can Say it All

- Ask your child to explain the *More than Words Can Express* activity used in the group. Using the table below to get started, create your own set of "task" and "feelings" cards to use at home. This activity works well as a fun family game or even an engaging pairs activity.

- Discuss how body language is used to express emotion, pointing out distinctive behaviors that you and your child observe in real-life situations.

- Make an ongoing game out of trying to guess what people may be talking about or how they are likely feeling, simply by observing their body language from afar. (Just be careful not to get caught staring!)

- Talk with your child about how learning to "read" body language can be a helpful way to understand how others are feeling in a situation.

- Use the *It's not the Words You Use but the Tone You Choose* handout with your child. Following the activity's directions, take turns saying the sentences with your child and talk about how the same words can express very different meaning, depending on the tone of voice and body language that accompanies it.

Copyright © Signe Whitson 2011

Part II
Developing Assertive Anger Expression Skills

Session 6

I Feel Angry!
Using I-Messages to Express Anger Assertively

Session objectives

- To understand how I-Messages are used to express anger assertively.
- To identify the essential elements of an effective I-Message.
- To practice constructing assertive I-Messages.

Materials needed

- pencils or pens for participants to use to complete written exercises
- index cards for the *I-Style* activity.

Before beginning

- Make question cards, as per the instructions from the *I-Style* activity (page 92).
- On flipchart paper, pre-print the I-Message template:

    I feel _____ (feeling) _____

    when _____ (describe behavior) _____

    because _____ (concrete effect or consequence on situation) ____

    I want _____ (describe desired behavior) _____

    I don't want ___ (describe behavior to be discontinued) _____

- Prepare copies of the *I-Messages* handout (page 94) for each participant.

- Prepare copies of the *You-Messages vs. I-Messages* handout (page 95) for each participant.

- Prepare copies of the *Sample I-Messages* handout (page 98) for each participant.

- Prepare copies of the *Weekly journal* (page 100) for each participant.

- Prepare copies of the *Notes for parents* handout (page 101) for each participant to take home.

Welcome back

1. Check in with participants on how they are using what they are learning in their day-to-day lives. If participants need prompts, ask:

    - *Has anyone found himself more likely to stop a destructive anger response and replace it with an assertive one?*

    - *Have you been noticing the choices others around you make when it comes to expressing anger?*

    - *Will anyone share a part of their journal and describe a person with whom they feel they can share their honest, inner feelings?*

2. *Over the first five group sessions, we have talked a lot about powerful feelings of anger and the choices we all make in how we express these feelings to the outside world, through our words and behaviors.*

3. *Now that we have established a common understanding of these things, we are going to turn our focus onto the* "What do I do to express anger effectively?" *question.*

4. *Over the next several sessions, we will be practicing specific skills for expressing anger (and other powerful emotions) assertively.*

5. *Today, we will be learning a skill called using "I-Messages" which is an assertive technique for honest communication and direct self-expression. To get you into the right frame of mind, we're going to start out today with a quick game in which pairs or groups of three participants practice sharing "I-Styles."*

Icebreaker activity: I-Style

1. Assign participants to work in pairs or groups of three.

2. Give each participant a question card from the *I-Style* activity (page 92). Their task is to interview the other person(s), using the question on their card.

3. Each question relates directly to a topic we have discussed so far in group and will give participants an opportunity to learn more about a fellow group member's personal style when it comes to anger expression.

4. Allow five minutes for participants to interview one another.

5. At the end of the activity, ask for 2–3 volunteers to share something that they learned they have in common with another participant, through this interview.

I-Messages

1. Ask participants if they have ever heard of the term "I-Messages" prior to this group session.

2. Explain that many people—not just kids—struggle with communicating powerful feelings effectively:

    *   *Even adults spend time practicing using I-Messages with each other, both in personal and professional relationships.*

    *   *I-Messages were developed to give people of all ages guidelines for assertive self-expression.*

3. Explain I-Messages in these terms: (this definition is included in the *I-Messages* handout (page 94) that can be distributed at the end of the session)

    *   *I-Messages model honest and direct anger expression. They are an essential tool of assertive self-expression because they allow a person to communicate their genuine thoughts and feelings in a respectful way that does not personally attack or tear down the other person. In a conflict situation, I-Messages aim to bring about needed change and resolve a problem.*

    *   *In contrast, You-Messages tend escalate conflict because they rely upon blame, shame, personal attacks, and put downs.*

4. Ask participants:

    *   *When you hear this definition of You-Messages, which of the four anger expression styles do you think of?*

    *   *Answer: You-Messages are an* aggressive *style of anger expression.*

5. *Though I-Messages can take many forms, the following template can be helpful when you first practice this style of assertive communication (refer to the pre-printed chart):*

I feel _____ (feeling) _____

when _____ (describe behavior) _____

because _____ (concrete effect or consequence on situation) _____

I want _____ (describe desired behavior) _____

I don't want _____ (describe behavior to be discontinued) _____

6. Provide these two examples as likely I-Messages that a teacher and child might use:

   Example 1: I feel concerned when I see you hitting your classmate because everyone here deserves a safe environment. I'd prefer for you to tell me about a situation that is bothering you and let me decide how to handle it. I don't want to see you acting out on your own in this way.

   Example 2: I feel angry when you take my Nintendo without asking because I am not allowed to let other people play with it when I'm not around. I want you to ask me before you play it. I don't want you to play when I'm not in the room or without asking me.

You-Messages vs. I-Messages

This activity will allow participants to practice turning potential conflicts into constructive communication by formulating assertive I-Messages.

1. Give each participant a copy of the *You-Messages vs. I-Messages* handout (page 95).

2. Ask participants to work in groups of 3–4.

3. Assign each small group to concentrate on a specific example from the worksheet. Depending on the size of your group, each group may be assigned 1–2 examples (there are five examples provided).

   • It can be very helpful to assign the same scenario to more than one group and to have participants reflect on the varied messages that each group generates.

   • This helps make the important point that even though we use the same general format to create I-Messages, the actual wording is not scripted. I-Messages vary as much as individuals do, but what they have in common is a non-blaming, respectful expression of feelings and needs.

4. Assign each group to read the scenario(s) and write down both an aggressive, conflict-fueling You-Message and an assertive, solution-focused I-Message.

5. Next, ask each group to develop a two-minute play that will illustrate both types of messages and their different consequences.

6. Allow ten minutes for small groups to work together, and then reconvene the large group.

7. Ask each group to read their scenario aloud, and then act out both the aggressive You-Message and the assertive I-Message.

8. After each play, ask participants for their comments, including:

   a. *What was the impact of the You-Message?*

      i. *How did it affect the conflict?*

      ii. *How did it affect the relationship between the two people?*

      iii. *Was the original problem solved?*

      iv. *How many problems now exist between the two people?*

   b. *What was the impact of the I-Message?*

      i. *How did it affect the conflict?*

      ii. *How did it affect the relationship between the two people?*

      iii. *Was the original problem solved?*

   c. *Why are I-Messages preferable to You-Messages when it comes to expressing anger?*

9. Affirm each small group role-play example and discussion, making sure to clarify and discuss correct responses.

10. Emphasize that the construction of I-Messages can be difficult at first!

   • The template makes I-Messages seem easy, but often people first learning the skill have difficulty adopting the true spirit of the messages.

   • For example, many kids might think that "I feel angry when you take my Nintendo because you are an as$%*le that can't be trusted and I don't want you to touch my stuff ever again" is an assertive I-Message, just because it begins with "I feel angry…"

This will be a challenging learning exercise for the participants and one that requires the facilitator to actively assist participants in how to correctly formulate a truly assertive I-Message.

11. If time permits, have the group develop a sixth possible scenario and, all together, come up with a destructive You-Message and an assertive I-Message. This concluding activity leaves participants with a relevant and clear example of an effective I-Message.

12. Conclude with an affirmation of how challenging I-Messages may seem at first, but ensure participants that with practice and repetition, these assertive responses are the ones that will be most constructive to forming positive friendships and getting the speaker's needs met.

13. Give each participant a copy of the *Sample I-Messages* (page 98) handout. Participants can refer back to this in the future as they are practicing I-Messages.

14. Remind participants:

    - *You have choices every day in how you respond to a situation.*

    - *You can choose to use aggressive "You-Statements" or assertive "I-Messages."*

    - *Your choices elicit predictable responses from others.*

    - *How you want people to treat you begins with how you treat others, including how you express angry thoughts and feelings.*

Session conclusion

1. *This week, we practiced a new skill for expressing thoughts and feelings in an assertive way.*

2. *Next week, we will continue to rely on I-Messages as we practice assertive skills for agreeing and disagreeing.*

3. Journal topic:

    - Write about a situation from the week in which you used an "I-Message" to communicate assertively. Use care in constructing the "I-Message" effectively.

    - If you used a "You-Message" instead, that's OK; this is a learning process and new habits don't come overnight. Use the journal to write the "You-Message," then below it, construct a more assertive "I-Message."

    - The purpose of this assignment is to reflect on your communication over the course of the week and practice using effective assertive "I-Messages" whenever possible.

Suggestions for customizing the curriculum

- Younger children may have difficulty using the question cards independently. Facilitators can instead conduct this activity as a large group, asking the questions aloud and calling on volunteers to answer them.

- Constructing effective I-Messages can be a difficult task, even for professional adults. Because I-Messages are a new way of communicating for many, the *I feel _____ when you _____ because_____* template often seems awkward at first. The facilitator should be very active throughout this session, offering support and reassurance to participants of all ages and abilities.

- If small groups are having an especially difficult time with the *You-Messages vs. I-Messages* activity, it may be helpful to work through the first 2–3 examples as a large group and to have the facilitator work with another adult to role-play several examples.

- For older or more sophisticated participants, assign small groups to work through one example from the *You-Messages vs. I-Messages* handout and then generate at least one original scenario and play.

- The weekly journal task is to write an effective I-Message. It does not provide a drawing option, as is normally given. If writing is not an option, suggest to participants that they either ask an adult to help them write the statement or they practice using an I-Message during the week and talk about it during the next group session.

Activity: I-Style

For the facilitator

- Before the group session begins, select different statements from the following list to print on question cards.

- At the start of the *I-Style* icebreaker activity, give each participant one question card.

- Working in pairs or groups of three, ask each participants to interview the other person(s), using the question on their card.

- The question cards will give participants an opportunity to learn more about a fellow group member's personal style when it comes to anger expression.

1. Are you more likely to lash out or withdraw when you are angry with someone? Give an example of a way you behaved last time you were feeling angry.	2. When you are angry, do you ever give the silent treatment? How long does it last? What happens when you start talking to the other person again?
3. Tell about a time when you felt one way on the inside, but acted differently on the outside.	4. What is a common trigger for your anger? How do you usually respond?
5. What is one current anger behavior pattern that you would like to change? What is the first step you can take to make a change?	6. Name one behavior you have used that was a passive way to express anger. How did it work for you?

Copyright © Signe Whitson 2011

7. Name one behavior you have used that was an aggressive way to express anger. How did the situation turn out?

8. Name one behavior you have used that was a passive aggressive way to express anger. How did it affect your relationship with the other person?

9. Tell about a time that you were able to express yourself assertively to someone else. How did it make you feel to assert your genuine thoughts and feelings in this way?

10. What kinds of non-verbal behaviors (body language and tone of voice) do you use? How do they get your message across to others?

11. What kinds of facial expressions do you use when you are angry? What does your voice sound like? How do your expressions and voice change when you are feeling happy?

12. Can someone tell you are angry just by looking at you? How?

13. Which level of passive aggressive behavior are you most likely to demonstrate?

14. Tell about a time that you used intentional inefficiency to express your anger in a passive aggressive way.

15. Tell about a time when you were passive aggressive with your parents. How did they respond? If you could do it all over again, would you choose to express your anger in a different way?

16. Describe a situation in which you were passive aggressive with a teacher. How did the teacher respond? If you could turn back time, would you choose to express your anger in a different way?

Copyright © Signe Whitson 2011

Handout: I-Messages

What are I-Messages?

I-Messages are an important tool of *assertive* communication. They are used to model honest and direct anger expression. I-Messages allow a person to express their thoughts and feelings in a respectful way that does not personally attack or tear down the other person.

What are the differences between I-Messages and You-Messages?

You-Messages are an *aggressive* style of anger expression. They use blame to express anger.

In a conflict situation, I-Messages aim to solve a problem while You-Messages usually make a problem worse because they rely upon blame, personal attacks, and put downs.

Effective I-Messages

Though I-Messages can take many forms, the following template can be helpful as you are first practicing this style of assertive communication:

I feel _____ (feeling) _____

when _____ (describe behavior) _____

because _____ (concrete effect or consequence on situation) ____

I want _____ (describe desired behavior) _____

I don't want ___ (describe behavior to be discontinued) _____

Example 1: I feel concerned when I see you hitting your classmate because everyone here deserves a safe environment. I'd prefer for you to tell me about a situation that is bothering you and let me decide how to handle it. I don't want to see you acting out on your own in this way.

Example 2: I feel angry when you take my Nintendo without asking because I am not allowed to let other people play with it when I'm not around. I want you to ask me before you play it. I don't want you to play when I'm not in the room or without asking me.

Note: The format for this I-Messages activity was originally developed by Gerrit De Moor. Adapted with permission.

     Copyright © Signe Whitson 2011

Handout: You-Messages vs. I-Messages

1. In small groups, read the assigned scenario(s), and then write down both an aggressive, conflict-fueling *You-Message* and an assertive, solution-focused *I-Message*.

2. Create a two-minute play to demonstrate both types of messages and their different results.

Scenarios

1. Last week, Jesse borrowed your favorite DVD. You have asked him for it back on two occasions and he keeps saying, "I'll bring it tomorrow." He forgot again today and you are feeling angry about it.

Copyright © Signe Whitson 2011

✓

2. Your mom is more than an hour late picking you up. She said she would meet you at 4pm, but she does not answer her cell phone and does not arrive until 5:15pm.

3. You privately texted your best friend about a guy you like. She showed the text to the guy! You are feeling humiliated.

Copyright © Signe Whitson 2011

4. Math is your worst subject, but you studied extra hard for a test and scored 100 percent. When your teacher hands it back to you, she smiles and says in front of the class, "Nice work, Jaime. Did you sneak a peek at my answer sheet ahead of time or something?" You are embarrassed and angry.

5. Several weeks ago, you and your friend Missy agreed to go to a party together on Halloween. You shopped for costumes together and talked about it all week. About an hour before the party, Missy calls to tell you that she won't be going to the party after all, because she is going to see a movie with her boyfriend.

Copyright © Signe Whitson 2011

Handout: Sample I-Messages

I-Messages can take many forms. In everyday usage, they do not follow a formula or a script. The page below provides one example of an effective I-Message for each of the conflict situations discussed in group. You will see that even though the template is not always followed in precise order, each essential part is fully covered in every I-Message.

Scenarios

1. Last week, Jesse borrowed your favorite DVD. You have asked him for it back on two occasions and he keeps saying, "I'll bring it tomorrow." He forgot again today and you are feeling angry about it.

   Assertive response: Jesse, I feel angry when you don't return my DVD because I haven't had the chance to watch it yet. I want you to keep your word and return it to me tomorrow. I don't want you to borrow my things and keep them as long as you want.

2. Your mom is more than an hour late picking you up. She said she would meet you at 4pm, but she does not answer her cell phone and does not arrive until 5:15pm.

   Assertive response: Mom, I am so relieved that you are here! I was really stressing about you not being on time. We agreed you'd pick me up by 4:00pm, but it is already a quarter past five. When you didn't call or answer your phone, I was really worried something bad had happened! Please stay in touch whenever you think you might be late. I don't want you to stay out of touch and leave me worried about where you might be.

3. You privately texted your best friend about a guy you like. She showed the text to the guy! You are feeling humiliated.

   Assertive response: Aimee, I sent you a text about Rod and you showed it to him. I feel totally hurt because the messages we send each other are private. I want you to keep the things we tell each other private. I don't want you to share things about me with Rod or anyone else.

Copyright © Signe Whitson 2011

4. Math is your worst subject, but you studied extra hard for a test and scored 100 percent. When your teacher hands it back to you, she smiles and says in front of the class, "Nice work, Jaime. Did you sneak a peek at my answer sheet ahead of time or something?" You are embarrassed and angry.

   Assertive response: Mrs. Thomas, I studied for three days straight for this math test. I felt embarrassed when you joked about me cheating in front of the whole class. Please hand my test grades back to me without saying anything in front of the class. I don't want you to share my test scores with others.

5. Several weeks ago, you and your friend Missy agreed to go to a party together on Halloween. You shopped for costumes together and talked about it all week. About an hour before the party, Missy calls to tell you that she won't be going to the party after all, because she is going to see a movie with her boyfriend.

   Assertive response: Missy, I feel angry when you cancel our plans at the last minute because I have been looking forward to going to this party with you. If you don't go, it will cancel my plans too. I want you to keep your promise to me. I don't want you to leave me hanging because you have better plans with your boyfriend.

Copyright © Signe Whitson 2011

Weekly journal

Write about a situation from the week in which you used an "I-Message" to communicate assertively. Use care in constructing the "I-Message" effectively.

If you used a "You-Message" instead, that's OK; this is a learning process and new habits don't come overnight. Use the journal to write the "You-Message," then below it, construct a more assertive "I-Message."

The purpose of this assignment is to reflect on your communication over the course of the week and practice using effective assertive "I-Messages" whenever possible.

Copyright © Signe Whitson 2011

Notes for parents from Session 6

I Feel Angry! Using I-Messages to Express Anger Assertively

- Ask your child to explain the *I-Style* activity used in the group. Using the topics below to get started, create a set of *I-Style* question cards to use at home. This question and answer activity can be a great family ritual after dinner or before bed. Parents should plan to participate in answering questions as well as asking them.

- Role modeling is the name of the game when it comes to helping kids work I-Messages into their normal self-expression patterns. The more parents demonstrate assertive communication, the easier it will be for kids to adopt these relationship-building patterns into their own life.

- Use the *You-Messages vs. I-Messages* handout with your child. Follow the activity's directions, constructive both the aggressive You-Messages and the assertive I-Messages. Role-play each one with your child.

- As situations come up in your everyday life, talk with your child about possible You-Messages vs. I-Messages that would be appropriate responses. Compare and contrast the potential effectiveness of both.

- Following a conflict, talk with your child about how the communication was handled and the type of words that were used. Ask your child to think about what was expressed effectively and what could have been phrased better.

Sample question topics from the I-Style activity, for at-home use:

1. Are you more likely to lash out, sulk, or withdraw when you are angry with someone? Give an example of a way you behaved last time you were feeling angry.

2. Tell about a time when you felt one way on the inside, but acted differently on the outside.

3. What is one current anger behavior pattern that you would like to change? What is the first step you can take to make a change?

Copyright © Signe Whitson 2011

4. Name one behavior you have used that was a passive way to express anger. How did it work for you?

5. Tell about a time that you were able to express yourself assertively to someone else. How did it make you feel to assert your genuine thoughts and feelings in this way?

6. What kinds of non-verbal behaviors (body language and tone of voice) do you use? How do they get your message across to others?

7. Can someone tell you are angry just by looking at you? How?

8. Describe a situation in which you were passive aggressive. How did the other person respond? If you could turn back time, would you choose to express your anger in a different way?

Copyright © Signe Whitson 2011

Yes, No, or Maybe So
Assertive Skills for Disagreeing without Arguing

Session objectives

- To understand key differences between arguing and disagreeing.
- To practice assertive skills for disagreeing without arguing.

Materials needed

- pencils or pens for participants to use to complete written exercises
- 11 x 14 inch (28 x 35 cm) poster board for *Yes, No or Maybe So* signs
- flipchart paper and markers.

Before beginning

- On flipchart paper, pre-print the *You-Messages* examples from the *Change It!* handout (page 109).
- Make *Yes, No* and *Maybe So* signs and post them in three separate areas around the room.
- Prepare copies of the *Change It!* handout (page 109) for each participant.
- Prepare copies of the *Weekly journal* (page 110) for each participant.
- Prepare copies of the *Notes for parents* handout (page 111) for each participant to take home.

Welcome back

1. Welcome participants back to the seventh session of group and check in with group members on how they are feeling before beginning.

2. Ask for a volunteer(s) to recall the "formula" for constructing an assertive "I-Message."

    I feel _____ when you _____ because _____.
    I want _____. I don't want _____.

3. Direct participants' attention to the "You-Messages" (from the *Change It!* handout on page 109), pre-printed on flipchart paper.

4. As a large group, call on volunteers to re-phrase the You-Message, replacing it with an assertive I-Message.

5. Remind participants that I-Messages help a person express feelings directly and build positive relationships.

Yes, No, or Maybe So

In your own words, convey the following introduction to this session's theme:

- *Every individual carries a unique set of opinions, beliefs, and perspectives about the world. From globally debated issues like politics and religion to everyday favorites in flavors of ice cream, personal preferences are part of what make people interesting!*

- *Sometimes, however, competing opinions cause hard feelings and anger.*

- *Today, we're going to talk about using assertive skills to express agreement and disagreement without expressing hostility.*

- *First, let's try a simple game. Around the room, you will see three signs, titled* Yes, No, *and* Maybe So. *I am going to read a simple statement aloud. If you agree with it, please walk over to the* Yes *sign. If you disagree with what I say, position yourself under the* No *sign. If you are really not sure or don't have a preference, you may choose to stand under the* Maybe So *sign.*

- *Let's begin:*

    Statement 1: Chocolate cake is better than apple pie any day.

    Statement 2: When I have free time, I like to play sports and be active.

    Statement 3: It's better to watch funny movies than scary ones.

Facilitators should feel free to add 1–2 additional statements, keeping the activity to no longer than ten minutes. The objective, at this point, is to use light-hearted, non-controversial statements.

Emphasize to participants that all people have varying opinions and preferences and that these differences need not have any bearing on how we feel about or towards each other.

> *These first few examples were really based on non-controversial, everyday likes and dislikes, but what happens when more heart-felt issues are at stake? How can we disagree with one another without arguing and damaging a friendship?*

Arguing vs. Disagreeing

1. Using flipchart paper, write the words *Arguing* and *Disagreeing* in two separate columns. Clarify that "arguing" usually occurs when two people consider each other's opinions invalid and wrong, while in a disagreement, people uphold their own point of view but maintain respect for the other person's opinion.

2. Ask participants to talk about the differences in behaviors that characterize arguing vs. disagreeing. For example, behaviors under the *Arguing* column might include:

    *   raising your voice, yelling, shouting (AG)

    *   cursing at the other person (AG)

    *   putting the other person's opinion down (AG)

    *   insulting the person on a personal level, "*You're so dumb. You don't even know what you are talking about*" (AG)

    *   interrupting (AG)

    *   using all-or-nothing exaggerations, such as "*always, never, evil, impossible*" (AG)

    *   sarcasm (PA)

    *   silent treatment (PA)

    *   sulking (PA).

    Behaviors under the *Disagreeing* column might include:

    *   looking the other person in the eyes when speaking

    *   using a calm, even tone of voice

- speaking at a regular volume

- using precise language rather than exaggerations

- respect

- friendliness

- accepting the other person's point of view as valid

- offering to "agree to disagree"

- thanking the person for their willingness to have a discussion.

3. After the list is complete, ask participants to look at their answers on the chart and identify each behavior as aggressive (AG), passive (P), passive aggressive (PA) or assertive (AS).

4. Emphasize that few (if any) of the behaviors listed will be passive, since most often passive people avoid both arguments and disagreements altogether. Recall that passive people believe that their opinions are not as worthy as those of the people around them so they actively avoid conflict.

5. Help participants contrast the effectiveness of aggressive and passive aggressive behaviors, which fall on the argumentative side, vs. the assertive ones that characterize disagreement. Ask:

- *Which set of behaviors is more likely to cause relationship-damaging wars of words?*

- *Which set of behaviors creates a climate of respect and mutual understanding?*

6. Tie in last session's skill development by reminding participants:

   I-Messages are a great assertive tool to use to express your point of view without arguing. In this next activity, see if you can work I-Messages into a disagreement.

7. Post sample topics and ask participants to work in pairs to practice first arguing, then disagreeing about the topic. (If there are an odd number of participants, have a group member work directly with a facilitator or rotate in with one of the pairs. Each round of argument of disagreement, however, should only involve two participants at once.)

8. Ask for 1–2 groups to volunteer to perform their argument and disagreement in front of the group.

9. Be sure to leave 5–10 minutes to process the role-plays and allow for further discussion, emphasizing:

- *Who "wins" in an argument?*

- *Who "wins" in a disagreement?*

- *Is "winning" important when it comes to differing opinions?*

- *How do you feel after an argument? After a disagreement?*

- *What are the benefits of using assertive communication skills in a disagreement over behaving aggressively or passive aggressively in an argument?*

- *Can you be angry without arguing?*

Session conclusion

1. *Differences of opinion are as natural as differences of hair and eye color. All humans develop their own set of thoughts, feelings, opinions, and perspectives. Assertive communication skills help us to* get along, *even when we can't* go along *with someone else's point of view.*

2. *Being friends with someone has nothing to do with agreeing all of the time, but has everything to do with disagreeing respectfully every time.*

3. Journal topic:

   - Think of a time in your life when you completely disagreed with someone else's opinion on a subject. How did that difference of opinion impact your relationship?

   - Is there a person in your life now with whom you frequently argue? How can you use assertive behaviors to change the tone of your interactions from relationship-damaging arguments to relationship-building disagreements?

   - There are no right or wrong answers when it comes to journaling. The purpose of this assignment is to think about using assertive skills to express disagreement without expressing hostility.

Suggestions for customizing the curriculum

- For younger participants who may not have been able to use last week's journal to write down effective I-Messages, allow time for discussion of situations over the last week in which I-Messages were used.

- Rather than being done as a large group activity, participants can be given a copy of the *Change It!* handout and assigned to work individually or in pairs on developing I-Messages. Answers can then be shared and compared as a large group.

- In the *Yes, No, or Maybe So* activity, customize the statements to match the interests and abilities of group participants.

- Younger participants may need the facilitator to take an active role in generating ideas and classifying behaviors as aggressive, passive, passive aggressive or assertive in the *Arguing vs. Disagreeing* activity. Older participants may be able to complete this activity with a large degree of independence. Consider allowing an older volunteer to "lead the discussion" by recording the answers on flipchart paper.

Handout: Change It!

In the examples below, change each statement from a conflict-fueling "You Message" to a solution-focused "I-Message."

1. You don't care about me. You're just talking to me because it's your job.

2. You are such a liar. You said you'd call and you didn't. Thanks a lot!

3. You are the worst friend ever. I'll never trust you with a secret again.

4. Get your hands off of my game. If you touch it again, I'll punch you in your face.

Copyright © Signe Whitson 2011

✓

Weekly journal

Write or draw about a time in your life when you completely disagreed with someone else's opinion on a subject. How did that difference of opinion impact your relationship?

Is there a person in your life now with whom you frequently argue? How can you use assertive behaviors to change the tone of your interactions from relationship-damaging arguments to relationship-building disagreements?

There are no right or wrong answers when it comes to journaling. The purpose of this assignment is to think about using assertive skills to express disagreement without expressing hostility.

Copyright © Signe Whitson 2011

Notes for parents from Session 7

Yes, No, or Maybe So: Assertive Skills for Disagreeing without Arguing

- Ask your child to tell you about the *Yes, No or Maybe So* activity used in group. This activity, designed to teach kids how to use assertive skills to express agreement and disagreement without expressing hostility, works well as a family game. Family members can take turns making up statements and expressing their opinions. Parents should validate the opinions and preferences of each family member and emphasize that differences should be celebrated as part of what makes each family member unique, rather than regarded as a source of conflict or hostility.

- Engage your kids in a conversation about the differences between "arguing" behaviors and "disagreeing" ones. Establish a set of family rules regarding the behaviors that can and cannot be used to express disagreement.

- When you observe conflict situations in the real world or on TV, talk with your kids about the ways in which people express disagreement. Ask kids to identify which behaviors express differences of opinion assertively versus which rely on aggression or passive aggression to argue and express hostility.

Copyright © Signe Whitson 2011

Keeping Bullies at Bay, Part 1
The Five Ws of Bullying

Session objectives

- To identify the five Ws of bullying.
- To reflect on examples and experiences of bullying behaviors in the lives of participants.

Materials needed

- soft ball or beanbag
- pencils or pens for participants to use to complete written exercises
- flipchart paper and markers.

Before beginning

- Prepare copies of *The Five Ws of Bullying* handout (page 118) for each participant.
- Prepare copies of *The Facts about the Five Ws of Bullying* handout (page 120) for each participant.
- Prepare copies of the *Weekly journal* (page 122) for each participant.
- Prepare copies of the *Notes for parents* handout (page 123) for each participant to take home.

Welcome back

Welcome participants to this eighth meeting, which marks the first of a two-part session on standing up to bullying. Say:

- *Over the next two sessions, we are going to tackle a topic that is on most kids' minds, most of the time: bullying!*

- *Today, we'll work as a group to get a clear picture of what bullies look like and how they operate. Next session, we'll practice four essential assertive communication skills for keeping bullies at bay.*

- *Before we begin this new topic, it will be helpful to revisit our last few, since the assertive skills we have practiced thus far are all essential tools for standing up to bullies effectively.*

Icebreaker activity: Toss It

1. *This is the eighth time we are meeting. We've reviewed four styles of anger expression and five levels of passive aggressive behavior. As a group, can you name at least six differences between arguing and disagreeing?*

2. Arrange participants in a standing up circle. Ask for a volunteer to go first, to name one example of a difference between arguing and disagreeing. Encourage examples that include ideas about body language, tone of voice, and I-Messages. Provide this example to clarify:

   In an argument, people often use personal attacks; in a disagreement, people stay focused on the issue itself.

3. Give the first volunteer a soft ball, bean bag, or other object that can be easily (and safely!) tossed. After he gives his example, ask him to carefully toss the object to another participant in the circle, who will then give his example.

4. Continue the activity in this way until each participant has had the chance to provide an example.

   - If a participant repeats something that has already been said, that's OK. Often, it is difficult for kids to think of novel responses "on the spot." The facilitator can make use of the repetition by acknowledging how important the example is.

   - Affirm each example and remind participants that the skills we have learned thus far in group are all important building blocks to learning about how to effectively stand up to bullies.

The Five Ws of Bullying

1. Explain to participants the following introductory points about bullying:

    *   *The bullies of today look, sound, and act differently from the bullies of your parents' and teachers' youth.*

    *   *Round-the-clock internet availability and 24/7 cell phone access has "revolutionized" the way that you communicate—both for better and for worse—and has made it more difficult for helpful adults to be aware that bullying is occurring.*

    *   *In the next session, we are going to talk more about your role in alerting adults when bullying is occurring, but, first, it's important for you to have a clear understanding of what a bully looks, sounds, and acts like.*

2. Give each participant a copy of *The Five Ws of Bullying* handout (page 118). In pairs or groups of three, assign participants to complete the form, describing in their own words the *who, what, when, where,* and *why* of bullying.

3. Remind participants that there are no wrong answers to this activity. Rather, the handout is designed to get participants thinking about the bullies in their world.

4. Allow 5–10 minutes for the small groups to share and record their responses, and then begin a group discussion.

5. The facilitator should take an active role in affirming the answers and personal experiences that are shared in this group session. The process of feeling heard and understood by peers about this weighty issue can be a very powerful experience for participants.

6. Allow plenty of time for the participants to share their answers, while also providing this supplemental information:

    *   What is bullying?

        *   According to the US Centers for Disease Control and Prevention, bullying occurs when a person or group repeatedly tries to harm someone who is weaker.

        *   Bully behavior takes many forms, from hitting, name calling, and teasing to social exclusion and rumor-spreading.

    *   Who is bullied?

        *   Bullies typically select targets who are unlikely to assert their rights and stand up for themselves.

- ◦ Studies show that children who are overweight, gay, or have disabilities (both physical and learning) are bullied at even higher rates.

- ◦ *If you have experienced bullying, you are not alone!*

This is a critical fact to reinforce to participants, since bullies strive to make their victims feel alone and powerless.

- • Where does bullying take place?

  - ◦ Traditionally, bullying centered in school settings, where kids had personal interactions throughout the academic day.

  - ◦ Today, internet access, social networking, video sharing sites, cell phones and text messaging have completely altered the landscape of bullying. No longer limited to face-to-face interactions, bullies can act out their aggression without having to look their victims in the eye. This wide-open access has made bullying more cruel and relentless than ever before.

- • When does bullying occur?

  - ◦ Likewise, bullying is no longer limited to the school day. Today, kids can't rely on their homes as safe havens from bullying, when technology allows for 24/7 interactions.

  - ◦ For those who are targeted by cruel peers, it can seem as if there is no escape from cruel teasing, taunting, and texting.

- • Why do people bully?

  - ◦ Bullies victimize others in order to gain power and control.

  - ◦ A bully's main objective is to make his victim feel alone and powerless.

  - ◦ Bullies are often people who feel very angry on the inside and have learned to express their feelings by lashing out and making others feel powerless.

7. Following the large group discussion, give each participant a copy of *The Facts about the Five Ws* handout (page 120).

Session conclusion

1. *Bullying is a major problem and persistent force in the lives of school-aged children. While it comes and goes in the media headlines, it is probably on your minds just about every day.*

2. *Thank you for your active participation and thoughtful responses today. As the old saying goes, "knowledge is power." The more we talk about bullying and bring these five Ws into everyday discussion, the more power we have to know what to do about it.*

3. *In the next session, we will continue the focus on bullying, learning four practical strategies for using assertive communication to stand up to bullies.*

4. Journal topic:

   - Write or draw about a time when you were bullied. Who was the bully? What did he/she do? How did he/she make you feel? How did you handle the situation? Who did you tell about the bullying?

   - Have you ever bullied someone else? What was causing your anger when you bullied? Have you had the chance to apologize to the person?

   - There are no right or wrong answers when it comes to journaling. The purpose of this assignment is to reflect on your own personal experiences with bullying.

Suggestions for customizing the curriculum

- Bullying is a topic that is relevant to most age groups and ability levels, so it is likely that all kids will have a lot to say on the subject matter. For younger participants, the facilitator might want to conduct the five Ws discussion as a large group, rather than breaking into small groups initially. Alternately, the facilitator may use five separate groups and ask each group to focus their responses on only one "W."

- For older participants with greater access to technology such as cell phones and social networking sites, it may be helpful to put greater emphasis on topics such as cyber-bullying.

Handout: The Five Ws of Bullying

In small groups, share your ideas and experiences about the following:

What is bullying?

Who is bullied?

Where does bullying take place?

Copyright © Signe Whitson 2011

When does bullying occur?

Why do people bully?

Copyright © Signe Whitson 2011

Handout: The Facts about the Five Ws of Bullying

What is bullying?

- According to the US Centers for Disease Control and Prevention, bullying occurs when a person or group repeatedly tries to harm someone who is weaker.

- Bully behavior takes many forms, from hitting, name calling, and teasing to social exclusion and rumor-spreading.

Who is bullied?

- Bullies typically select targets that are unlikely to assert their rights and stand up for themselves.

- Studies show that children who are overweight, gay, or have disabilities (both physical and learning) are bullied at even higher rates.

- If you have experienced bullying, you are not alone!

Where does bullying take place?

- Traditionally, bullying centered in school settings, where kids had personal interactions throughout the academic day.

- Today, internet access, social networking, video sharing sites, cell phones and text messaging have completely altered the landscape of bullying. No longer limited to face-to-face interactions, bullies can act out their aggression without having to look their victims in the eye. This wide-open access has made bullying more cruel and relentless than ever before.

Copyright © Signe Whitson 2011

When does bullying occur?

- Likewise, bullying is no longer limited to the school day. Today, kids can't rely on their homes as safe havens from bullying, when technology allows for 24/7 interactions.

- For those who are targeted by cruel peers, it can seem as if there is no escape from cruel teasing, taunting, and texting.

Why do people bully?

- Bullies victimize others in order to gain power and control.

- A bully's main objective is to make his/her victim feel alone and powerless.

- Bullies are often people who feel very angry on the inside and have learned to express their feelings by lashing out and making others feel powerless.

Copyright © Signe Whitson 2011

Weekly journal

Write or draw about a time when you were bullied. Who was the bully? What did he/she do? How did he/she make you feel? How did you handle the situation? Who did you tell about the bullying?

Have you ever bullied someone else? What was causing your anger when you bullied? Have you had the chance to apologize to the person?

There are no right or wrong answers when it comes to journaling. The purpose of this assignment is to reflect on your own personal experiences with bullying.

Copyright © Signe Whitson 2011

Notes for parents from Session 8

Keeping Bullies at Bay, Part 1: The Five Ws of Bullying

- It is important for parents to be as open to learning about bullying as kids are. Talk with your child about the five Ws of bullying, using the handout from the group as your guide.

- Since the bullies of today use such different methods than the bullies of parents' youth, it is helpful for parents to engage in consistent dialogue with their kids about friends, friendships, elements of healthy and unhealthy peer relationships, and any bullying issues that they know about and/or experience personally.

- Believe your child when he/she talks to you about bullying. This creates an open door for important discussions.

- It may be tempting for parents to tell kids to simply "not worry about" seemingly minor issues or to advise kids against "tattling" to adults. Resist the urge to "solve" the issue in this way. Instead, allow your child to use you as a sounding board for talking about the relationship issues on his/her mind.

- Use television news stories and magazine or online articles about real-life bullying incidents to reinforce the information from the group and to teach your child new facts about bullies. Knowledge truly is power and when kids are able to identify bullying behaviors, they are in the best position to stand up to bullies assertively.

- For additional skills and at-home discussion starter ideas, please check out *Friendship and Other Weapons: Group Activities to Help Young Girls Aged 5–11 to Cope with Bullying* (Whitson 2012).

Copyright © Signe Whitson 2011

Keeping Bullies at Bay, Part 2

Four Rules for Using Assertive Communication to Stand Up to Bullies

Session objectives

- To learn four rules for standing up to bullying behaviors.
- To identify key differences between effective and ineffective responses to bullies.
- To practice using assertiveness skills to stand up to bullying behavior.

Materials needed

- flipchart paper and markers
- 11 x 14 inch (28 x 35 cm) poster board to feature the four "Don't" rules.

Before beginning

- Pre-print the phrase "Too powerful to provoke" on a flipchart.
- Pre-print the four "Don't" rules on the poster board.
- Prepare copies of *Seven Truths and Three Lies for Standing Up to Bullies* handouts 1–4 (pages 131–135) for each participant.
- Prepare copies of *Four Rules for Using Assertive Communication to Stand Up to Bullies* handout (page 136) for each participant.

- Select three volunteers from the group and practice the assigned role-play from the *Putting It All Together* activity (page 139). Give each volunteer a copy of this activity sheet.

- Prepare copies of the *Too Powerful to Provoke—Role-Plays for Practicing Assertive Communication* handout (page 140) for each participant.

- Prepare copies of the *Weekly journal* (page 145) for each participant.

- Prepare copies of the *Notes for parents* handout (page 146) for each participant to take home.

Welcome back

1. Welcome participants back to the second half of the group's two-part discussion on bullying.

    - *Last week, we focused on the five Ws of bullying, including what, who, where, when, and why bullying occurs.*

    - *Does anyone remember what we discussed as the bully's primary goal?*

      Answer: To make victims feel alone and powerless.

    - *Who recalls the overall feature that most bullies look for when selecting their targets?*

      Answer: Kids who do not assert their rights or stand up for themselves.

    - *The more bullies confirm that they can pick on their target unchecked, the more they will do it. That's why an assertive response is so effective in countering bullying; the child who masters assertive communication demonstrates that a bully's attacks will be answered in a fair, but formidable way. Finding their target to be* too powerful to provoke, *bullies will most often move on.*

2. It may be helpful to write the phrase "Too powerful to provoke" on a sheet of flipchart paper prior to the group's beginning, so that the phrase can linger in the participants' minds throughout the session.

    Today, we are going to talk about four strategies for using assertive communication to stand up to bullies effectively.

Icebreaker activity: Two Truths and a Lie

1. Tell participants that to get started today, you will be playing a fun game called *Two Truths and a Lie*.

2. In this game, each participant takes a turn saying three sentences about himself, two of which are factually correct, and one of which is a lie. Listeners have to try to identify the untrue statement.

3. The facilitator should begin the game, to role model the process. Provide a personal example such as:

   - My birthday is in May. (True)

   - I love to eat pretzels. (True)

   - I am left-handed. (False)

4. Encourage participants to generate "low-risk" statements for the fun of the game, rather than getting into personal disclosure for this activity.

5. Allow everyone to have a turn creating statements for others to guess. If any participant chooses to "pass" on participating, this is OK. Some participants may feel shy about creating statements, though they may still enjoy the process of guessing other people's truths and lies.

6. Once each participant has had the chance to take a turn, summarize that group members are getting to know one another better and learning new, interesting facts about each other through the process of the group. As friendships and bonds form, group members are learning and practicing important new skills together.

Four Rules for Standing Up to Bullies

1. *Today, we are going to talk about four rules for using assertive communication to stand up to bullying behavior.*

2. *Since bullying is something we don't want to stand for, each rule starts with the word, "Don't." Simply put, the rules are:*

   - Don't go it alone.

   - Don't wait.

   - Don't beat around the bush.

   - Don't mix signals.

3. As each rule is read aloud, hold up the pre-printed "Don't" posters as visual cues.

4. Divide participants into four small groups. Hand each group one of the signs, along with the *Seven Truths and Three Lies for Standing Up to Bullies* handout (pages 131–135) that corresponds to their "Don't" rule.

5. On the handout, participants will find seven true statements that support or explain their "Don't" rule, along with three statements that are false and don't belong.

6. Participants should work within their small groups to identify the "lies."

7. Once they have identified all of the false statements, each group will present the true ones to the rest of the large group, in four separate presentations.

   Answer—the false statements are as follows:

   • *Rule 1*: 3, 7, 9

   • *Rule 2*: 4, 7, 9

   • *Rule 3*: 3, 5, 8

   • *Rule 4*: 3, 4, 6

8. Allow approximately five minutes for the small groups to identify the statements as true or false, providing guidance as requested.

9. Allow approximately 10–15 minutes for the four groups to present their information and discuss their answers.

10. The facilitator should affirm each group's answers while making sure that the true statements have been correctly identified. Elaborate on any discussion points that need clarification or explanation.

11. Once the presentations and discussion are complete, Facilitator should give each participant a copy of the *Four Rules for Using Assertive Communication to Stand Up to Bullies* handout (page 136) that lists all of the correct statements under each "Don't" rule.

Putting It All Together: Role-Playing

1. Prior to the group session, the facilitator should select three group members and assign each a role based on the first example in the *Too Powerful to Provoke—Role-Plays for Practicing Assertive Communication* handout (page 140).

2. The facilitator should play the role of the bully and allow each pre-selected group member to present their assigned response (passive, aggressive, or assertive) to the bully's statement.

3. Group members will be challenged to identify which two approaches are ineffective (the passive and aggressive ones) and why. Encourage answers along the lines of:

   - The aggressive approach is ineffective because it invites further conflict.

   - The passive approach is ineffective because it allows the bully to trample over the victim's boundaries.

   - The assertive approach is effective because it is simple, unemotional, and to the point.

4. After group members correctly identify and discuss the assertive approach in this example, they should return to their small groups and work on the remaining examples in the *Too Powerful to Provoke—Role-Plays for Practicing Assertive Communication* handout. Each group should be assigned to create passive, aggressive, and assertive responses to a specific scenario or, if time permits, to each one.

5. Remind participants to incorporate knowledge from past sessions, such as using body language and tone of voice cues, in their role-plays.

6. Allow enough time at the end of the session for at least two groups to present their role-plays, while other group members identify the effective assertive approach.

7. Reassure participants that formulating assertive responses to bullying can be tricky for kids, especially when they are first learning the skill.

   Whenever a person learns a new skill, the words feel awkward at first. Remember how strange it felt at first to use I-Messages in Session 6? If practiced often, assertive responses can quickly become second nature.

8. Be sure to affirm each small group's role-play while also clarifying effective assertive responses.

Session conclusion

1. *This week, we focused on four rules for using assertive communication to stand up to bullies. We practiced becoming too powerful to provoke.*

2. *Assertive communication is the essential middle ground between an aggressive comeback that escalates a bully's hostility and a passive response that reveals a target's lack of power.*

3. *Kids who master assertive communication demonstrate that a bully's attacks will be answered in a fair, but formidable way. Finding his target to be too powerful to provoke, the bully will most often move on.*

4. *Feeling comfortable with the power of assertive communication does not usually happen for kids right away, but, with time and practice, all kids can develop the skills to effectively keep bullies at bay.*

5. Journal topic:

   Bully behavior occurs all around kids, every day. This week, be extra alert to the bullying in your world. When you witness a bullying situation, write or draw about it in your journal.

   - What was the scenario?
   - How did the bully's target respond?
   - Was his response passive, aggressive or assertive?
   - Was the response effective?
   - If not, suggest a more effective, assertive response.

Suggestions for customizing the curriculum

- Younger participants may do better with fewer than ten statements in the *Seven Truths and Three Lies* activity. Prior to the group, the facilitator may eliminate some statements and/or adjust the language so that it works for the reading level of the participants.

- During the role-play activities, younger participants may benefit from having the facilitator provide hints and suggestions for developing each type of response.

- Older participants may be challenged to develop original role-play scenarios.

- Across all age groups, it is likely that participants will have personal examples and experiences to share about bullying. While the role-plays are helpful, real-life experiences can be even more valuable for the group to discuss and work through. Whenever possible, utilize members' examples as part of the group discussion and role-play.

Handout: Seven Truths and Three Lies about Standing Up to Bullies (1)

Can you spot the three lies for Rule 1?

Rule 1: Don't go it alone

1. A bully's main strategy is to make a victim feel alone and powerless.

2. The best way to counter a bully's strategy is to tell a helpful adult about what is going on and ask for that adult's support. When a bully realizes that he/she will not be able to keep a victim isolated—that the victim is strong enough to reach out and connect with others—the bully begins to lose power.

3. Kids shouldn't tell adults about bullying. Adults never do anything—so why even bother?

4. Sometimes adults fail to acknowledge the seriousness of bullying, but, more often, grown-ups are not aware of what is going on.

5. These days, bullies use the internet and other behind-the-scenes ways to hurt others that tend not to be noticed by adults.

6. It is a kid's job to create awareness in adults about bullying.

7. Telling an adult about bullying is a mark of cowardice.

8. Telling an adult about bullying is a bold, powerful move.

9. Bullying will worsen if you tattle to an adult.

10. Bullies want their victims to be too afraid to tell an adult about what is going on. That's why they tease kids about "tattling." See right through their game! This is just another one of the bully's strategies for intimidating you and making you feel all alone.

Copyright © Signe Whitson 2011

Handout: Seven Truths and Three Lies about Standing Up to Bullies (2)

Can you spot the three lies for Rule 2?

Rule 2: Don't wait!

1. Kids should tell adults about bullying and ask for an adult's support.

2. The longer a bully has power over a victim, the stronger the hold becomes.

3. Bullying usually begins in a relatively mild form—name calling, teasing, or minor physical aggression—then becomes more serious when the bully realizes that his/her victim is not going to stand up for him/herself.

4. If a bully thinks his/her victim will not fight back, he/she usually moves on to someone else who is better at standing up for him/herself and asserting his/her rights.

5. When kids let bullying behavior go on unchecked, their own power slips away steadily.

6. Taking action against the bully—and taking it sooner rather than later—is the best way to gain and retain power.

7. Telling an adult about bullying is tattling. Kids should handle bullies on their own.

8. Telling an adult about bullying is a bold, powerful move.

9. Kids should tell their parents about bullies but they shouldn't involve teachers or other non-family members.

10. If a kid is being bullied, he/she should tell an adult who can be helpful in the situation. Sometimes a parent will be the most helpful, but other times a school teacher, neighbor, counselor, or other adult friend might be in the best position to help.

Copyright © Signe Whitson 2011

Handout: Seven Truths and Three Lies about Standing Up to Bullies (3)

Can you spot the three lies for Rule 3?

Rule 3: Don't beat around the bush!

1. The more a bully thinks he/she can pick on a victim without a direct response, the more he/she will do it.

2. Assertiveness is the essential middle ground between aggressive comebacks that invite further conflict and passive responses that allow personal boundaries to be violated.

3. Abby: Where'd you get your outfit—the clearance rack?

   Jen: Yeah, my mom made me wear it. I love what you have on, though. You always look so awesome.

   Jennifer's response is effective. She compliments Abby and tries to make friends with her.

4. Abby: Where'd you get your outfit—the clearance rack?

   Jen: Yeah, my mom made me wear it. I love what you have on, though. You always look so awesome.

   Jennifer's response is ineffective. By complimenting Abby after such an obvious put down, Jennifer allows her power to be drained. She is basically saying, "Reject me again, hurt me some more. Whatever you say is OK because I am just so desperate to be liked."

5. Abby: Where'd you get your outfit—the clearance rack?

   Jen: I got it out of your closet, loser.

   Jennifer's response is effective. Her snappy comeback lets Abby know that she is ready and willing to fight. It is helpful to challenge bullies and make them prove what they are made of.

Copyright © Signe Whitson 2011

6. Abby: Where'd you get your outfit—the clearance rack?

    Jen: I got it out of your closet, loser.

    Jennifer's response is ineffective. It challenges Abby to escalate her aggression. Snappy, humiliating comebacks invite bullies to keep the conflict going and turn up the heat for the next round.

7. Abby: Where'd you get your outfit—the clearance rack?

    Jen: Knock it off, Abby.

    Jennifer's response is effective. She uses assertive communication to let Abby know that she does not intend to be victimized. Jennifer does not seek forgiveness, but does not pose a challenge either. Her response is simple and unemotional.

8. Abby: Where'd you get your outfit—the clearance rack?

    Jen: Knock it off, Abby.

    Jennifer's response is ineffective. This simple assertive statement is too straightforward. It's better to be indirect with bullies and keep them guessing about whether or not you will be able to stand up for yourself.

9. Simple, unemotional responses are effective in standing up to bullies because they portray confidence.

10. Emotional responses signal to a bully that he/she will be able to take control of a situation and gain power over the victim.

Copyright © Signe Whitson 2011

Handout: Seven Truths and Three Lies about Standing Up to Bullies (4)

Can you spot the three lies for Rule 4?

Rule 4: Don't mix signals!

1. Assertive responses combine the use of direct words with assertive body language and tone of voice.

2. Use a calm, even tone of voice when talking to a bully. This shows confidence.

3. Shouting and cursing at a bully are helpful, aggressive ways to show a bully that you are not afraid of a fight.

4. Shouting and cursing are helpful when talking to a bully because they portray confidence. Usually, being louder than the bully de-escalates a conflict.

5. Stand an appropriate distance from the bully. This shows that you are not easily intimidated.

6. "Getting in a bully's face" is a good way to show the bully that you are not scared of him/her.

7. Avoiding eye contact with a bully is an unhelpful response. It signals that you don't respect yourself and likely will not stand up for your rights.

8. Look a bully directly in the eye. Maintaining eye contact is a mark of emotionally honest and direct communication.

9. Use the bully's name when responding to insults. This is an assertive technique that lets the bully know he/she is your equal.

10. Emotional body language, such as looking away, raising your voice, or shrinking back are all dead giveaways that the bully has intimidated you.

Copyright © Signe Whitson 2011

Handout: Four Rules for Using Assertive Communication to Stand Up to Bullies

Rule 1: Don't go it alone

1. A bully's main strategy is to make a victim feel alone and powerless.

2. The best way to counter a bully's strategy is to tell a helpful adult about what is going on and ask for that adult's support. When a bully realizes that he/she will not be able to keep a victim isolated—that the victim is strong enough to reach out and connect with others—the bully begins to lose power.

3. Sometimes adults fail to acknowledge the seriousness of bullying, but more often, grown-ups are not aware of what is going on.

4. These days, bullies use the internet and other behind-the-scenes ways to hurt others that tend not to be noticed by adults.

5. It is a kid's job to create awareness in adults about bullying.

6. Telling an adult about bullying is a bold, powerful move.

7. Bullies want their victims to be too afraid to tell an adult about what is going on. That's why they tease kids about "tattling." See right through their game! This is just another one of the bully's strategies for intimidating you and making you feel all alone.

Rule 2: Don't wait!

1. Kids should tell adults about bullying and ask for an adult's support.

2. The longer a bully has power over a victim, the stronger the hold becomes.

3. Bullying usually begins in a relatively mild form—name calling, teasing, or minor physical aggression—then becomes more serious when the bully realizes that the victim is not going to stand up for him/herself.

4. When kids let bullying behavior go on unchecked, their own power slips away steadily.

Copyright © Signe Whitson 2011

5. Taking action against the bully—and taking it sooner rather than later—is the best way to gain and retain power.

6. Telling an adult about bullying is a bold, powerful move.

7. If a kid is being bullied, they should tell an adult who can be helpful in the situation. Sometimes a parent will be the most helpful, but other times a school teacher, neighbor, counselor, or other adult friend might be in the best position to help.

Rule 3: Don't beat around the bush!

1. The more bullies think they can pick on a victim without a direct response, the more they will do it.

2. Assertiveness is the essential middle ground between aggressive comebacks that invite further conflict and passive responses that allow personal boundaries to be violated.

3. Abby: Where'd you get your outfit—the clearance rack?

   Jen: Yeah, my mom made me wear it. I love what you have on, though. You always look so awesome.

   Jen's response is ineffective. By complimenting Abby after such an obvious put-down, Jen allows her power to be drained. She is basically saying, "Reject me again, hurt me some more. Whatever you say is OK because I am just so desperate to be liked."

4. Abby: Where'd you get your outfit—the clearance rack?

   Jen: I got it out of your closet, loser.

   Jen's response is ineffective. It challenges Abby to escalate her aggression. Snappy, humiliating comebacks invite bullies to keep the conflict going and turn up the heat for the next round.

5. Abby: Where'd you get your outfit—the clearance rack?

   Jen: Knock it off, Abby.

   Jen's response is effective. She uses assertive communication to let Abby know that she does not intend to be victimized. Jen does not seek forgiveness, but does not pose a challenge either. Her response is simple and unemotional.

Copyright © Signe Whitson 2011

6. Simple, unemotional responses are effective in standing up to bullies because they portray confidence.

7. Emotional responses signal to bullies that they will be able to take control of a situation and gain power over their victims.

Rule 4: Don't mix signals!

1. Assertive responses combine the use of direct words with assertive body language and tone of voice.

2. Use a calm, even tone of voice when talking to a bully. This shows confidence.

3. Stand an appropriate distance from the bully. This shows that you are not easily intimidated.

4. Avoiding eye contact with a bully is an unhelpful response. It signals that you don't respect yourself and likely will not stand up for your rights.

5. Look a bully directly in the eye. Maintaining eye contact is a mark of emotionally honest and direct communication.

6. Use the bully's name when responding to one of his/her insults. This is an assertive technique that lets the bully know he/she is your equal.

7. Emotional body language, such as looking away, raising your voice, or shrinking back are all dead giveaways that the bully has intimidated you.

Copyright © Signe Whitson 2011

Activity: Putting It All Together

For the facilitator

Prior to the session, select three group members to participate in a brief demonstration. Assign each person to play one of the versions of "Tess" described below. Follow the instructions in the "Putting It All Together: Role-Playing" section on pages 128–129.

Group role-play example

Abby: *If you want to sit at our table, you can't dress like that. You have to wear clothes from the mall.*

Tess: *These are from the mall. They're from your favorite store. I love the way you dress.*

This response is a *passive* one that allows Abby to trample over Tess' personal boundaries. By complimenting Abby after her obvious attempt at exclusion, Tess sends a clear message: "Insulting me is OK. Demeaning me is just fine. I will tolerate whatever you say, in hopes that you will like me."

Tess: *Who would want to sit here with you at the loser table, anyway?*

This *aggressive* response challenges Abby to up the ante on the conflict. While snappy comebacks sound and feel good in the moment, in the long run, they are the classic example of two wrongs spiraling toward disaster. By mirroring Abby's aggressive response, Tess has virtually guaranteed that another conflict will ensue.

Tess: *Cut it out, Abby. Clothes aren't what's really important here.*

This response is *assertive*. Tess lets Abby know that she does not intend to be victimized. Her communication is simple and unemotional. It protects her boundaries without trampling over Abby's.

This role-play is based on the bullying tactic of social exclusion.

Copyright © Signe Whitson 2011

Handout: Too Powerful to Provoke—Role-Plays for Practicing Assertive Communication

1. Read the bullying scenarios below.

2. Identify a possible passive, aggressive, and assertive response to each scenario.

3. Be prepared to present your role-play, challenging other group members to correctly identify the assertive approach.

4. In your role-play, be sure to incorporate knowledge from past sessions, such as using body language, tone of voice, and I-Messages to reinforce your words.

Role-play 1

At school, you notice that all of the kids at school are laughing and whispering whenever you walk by. Your best friend tells you that Connor, a boy who has been teasing you all year long, used his MySpace page to spread a cyber-rumor about you. In under 24 hours, the rumor has spread throughout your school.

Passive response:

Copyright © Signe Whitson 2011

Aggressive response:

Assertive response:

This role-play is based on cyber-bullying and rumor spreading.

Copyright © Signe Whitson 2011

Role-play 2

Every day in the school cafeteria line, Gwen taunts Courtney about her size, her appetite, and her elastic-waist pants. Today, Gwen comments, "I see they are serving your perfect meal, Courtney—a 'plump' hot dog."

Passive response:

Aggressive response:

Assertive response:

This role-play is based on verbal aggression, including name-calling and taunting.

Copyright © Signe Whitson 2011

Role-play 3

Richie is constantly picked on by his classmate, Will. Yesterday, Will knocked Richie's books off of his desk, scattering his papers all over the floor just as class was about to begin and humiliating Richie in the process. This morning, Will keyed the paint on Richie's car door in the school parking lot. At lunch, Will stuck his foot out to trip Richie just as his arms were full with his lunch tray and drink. Richie fell flat on his face in front of the entire lunchroom.

Passive response:

Aggressive response:

Assertive response:

This role-play is based on physical aggression, including tripping and destruction of property.

Role-play 4

Carly is angry at Becca for texting a note to her boyfriend. Even though Becca showed Carly the note to prove to her that the conversation was only about science homework, Carly is still upset. She gives Becca the silent treatment for the rest of the week and convinces Becca's two closest friends to do the same.

Passive response:

Aggressive response:

Assertive response:

This role-play is based on relational aggression, including giving Becca the silent treatment and manipulating her peer relationships.

Copyright © Signe Whitson 2011

Weekly journal

Bully behavior occurs all around kids, every day. This week, be extra alert to the bullying in your world. When you witness a bullying situation, write or draw about it in your journal. Include elements such as:

- What was the scenario?

- How did the bully's target respond?

- Was his/her response passive, aggressive, or assertive?

- Was the response effective?

- If not, suggest a more effective, assertive response.

The purpose of this journaling activity is to help you think about assertive responses to bullying.

Copyright © Signe Whitson 2011

Notes for parents from Session 9

Keeping Bullies at Bay, Part 2: Four Rules for Using Assertive Communication to Stand Up to Bullies

- Have an open door policy when it comes to allowing your child to talk to you about issues related to friendships and bullying. The more kids feel like they can talk to their parents about peer relationships, the more they will trust parents with information about bullying behavior.

- As noted last session, it is critical that parents believe what their kids tell them about bullying and do not minimize the issues. When kids know that their family members will take their concerns seriously, they feel safe enough to reach out for help in a timely way.

- As real-life bullying situations come up or are seen on TV, use role-play with your child to work through possible responses (passive, aggressive, assertive). Talk about likely outcomes of each response.

- Reinforce to your child that *he/she is never alone* when it comes to asserting him/herself with a bully. It's never too early to make a plan for who your child can talk to about bullying and how to respond assertively to bullying behavior.

Copyright © Signe Whitson 2011

Session 10

"May I Please" and "No Can Do"
Guidelines for Assertively Making and Refusing Requests

Session objectives

- To learn and practice two key guidelines for making requests assertively.
- To learn and practice four important rules for refusing requests assertively.
- To practice using assertiveness skills to say "No."

Materials needed

- pencil or pen to complete written exercises.

Before beginning

- Prepare copies of *May I Please—Two Simple Rules for Making Assertive Requests* handout (page 152) for each participant.

- Prepare copies of *No Can Do—Four Rules for Refusing Requests Assertively* handout (page 155) for each participant.

- (Optional) Prepare copies of the *Suggested Answer Guide* handout (page 157) for each participant.

- Prepare copies of the *Assertive Dos and Don'ts of Saying "No"* handout (page 158) for each participant.

- Prepare copies of the *Weekly journal* (page 159) for each participant.

- Prepare copies of the *Notes for parents* handout (page 160) for each participant to take home.

Welcome back

1. Welcome participants back to the tenth group session. Affirm how many skills participants have already practiced (it may be useful to call on a volunteer(s) to name a few) and emphasize the important learning that took place over the last two sessions, in developing assertive behaviors for standing up to bullies.

2. Preview that in this session, we are going to focus on a skill that is often difficult for people with passive styles: Making and refusing requests.

Icebreaker activity: Say the Alphabet

In this activity, the group needs to work together to achieve a seemingly simple task. The goal is often more difficult than it would seem, but the objective is for participants to use non-verbal communication and persistence to work together to say the alphabet from A to Z.

1. Tell participants the rules:

   - *Your group goal is to say the alphabet by having different group members say individual letters aloud, in sequence, from A to Z.*

   - *The catch is that the only words that can be spoken are the letters themselves and that if two people speak at the same time, the group has to start over from the letter A.*

2. There are many "easy" ways to do this, such as non-verbally signaling for one person to begin and then continuing in order around the seating pattern. However, it usually takes a few rounds for groups to figure out how to create an orderly way of taking turns and communicating well in order to complete the task.

3. Briefly discuss how non-verbal communication and teamwork came into play during this activity.

Making Requests

1. In your own words, convey the following introduction to the lesson:

    *   *For some people, communicating basic needs and making direct requests is a real challenge.*

    *   *People who use a passive communication style often believe that their needs are not worthy of consideration or that their feelings are not as important as those of others. As a result, they communicate their needs, wants, and feelings in indirect ways.*

    *   *Nonetheless, passive people have real emotions, such as anger, and real needs, just like all of the rest of us. When people with a passive style learn assertive skills for communicating anger and making/refusing requests, they become better able to develop more honest, positive relationships.*

2. Give each participant a copy of the *May I Please—Two Simple Rules for Making Assertive Requests* handout (page 152).

3. Explain that there are just two simple guidelines when it comes to making assertive requests. Ask for a volunteer to read the rules aloud:

    *   State the request.

    *   Be persistent.

4. In small groups, ask participants to read the need expressed in each item on the handout (e.g. *Help with homework*) and to write a request according to the styles indicated.

5. Allow five minutes for participants to complete the assignment, and then reconvene as a large group to review answers.

6. Use the following questions to guide the discussion:

    *   *What are the problems with the passive and aggressive requests?*

    *   *Would you want someone to approach you, using a passive or aggressive style?*

    *   *Do passive and aggressive styles make relationships better or worse? Explain?*

    *   *What is it about an assertive style that makes you more likely to get what you want?*

    *   *How does assertive communication build relationships?*

7. Affirm all answers while clarifying effective responses so that participants gain a good understanding of how to make assertive requests.

8. Emphasize the following:

- *Along with your right to make a request comes another person's right to refuse your request.*

- *Learning how to assertively communicate a request does not always guarantee that you will get exactly what you want, when you want it. That is not the goal of assertive communication, however.*

- *Rather, the goal is to for you to be able to express yourself in an emotionally honest, direct way and to build meaningful relationships with others.*

Refusing Requests

- *Not only do you have the right to make requests, but you have the right to refuse unreasonable requests from others.*

- *In fact, saying "no" can be healthy when it prevents you from being controlled by others, taken advantage of, overwhelmed, or when it helps you steer clear of potential trouble.*

- *What's more, you have the right to refuse a request without feeling guilty. Guilt is an emotion often experienced by people with passive communication styles. It motivates them to prioritize other people's wants over their own rights and needs.*

1. Give each participant a copy of the *No Can Do—Four Rules for Refusing Requests Assertively* handout (page 155).

2. Ask for a volunteer to read aloud the four guidelines for assertively refusing requests:

   - Be direct, firm, and honest when refusing a request.

   - Ask for more information if you are not sure what the request involves.

   - Postpone giving an answer if you need more time to consider the request.

   - Use I-Messages to express your feelings assertively if the other person tries to force you into granting their request.

3. Ask participants to work individually or in pairs to look at the eight sentences at the bottom of the *No Can Do—Four Rules for Refusing Requests Assertively* handout and identify whether the sentence is passive, assertive, or aggressive. If it is passive or aggressive, ask participants to rewrite the statement to make it more assertive.

4. Allow 5–10 minutes for the activity, and then reconvene the group to review the correct style identifications and suggestions for assertive refusals. A *Suggested Answer Guide* (page 157) is provided for the facilitator. As an option, this may be distributed to participants following the discussion.

5. Summarize the session by reminding participants that the ability to make and refuse requests assertively is a key element in emotionally honest, direct communication and in building positive, meaningful relationships.

6. Give each participant a copy of the *Assertive Dos and Don'ts of Saying "No"* handout (page 158), as a summary and review tool.

Session conclusion

1. *This week, we focused on making and refusing requests in an assertive style.*

2. *Next week, we'll revisit these skills and also talk about giving and receiving compliments assertively.*

3. Journal topic:

   - This week, take special note of the way that you, and those around you, approach asking for what you want and need. Practice making requests assertively and journal about the occasions that you did so, using the assertive words you chose.

   - Feel free to also journal about the passive and aggressive requests that you observe in your day to day activities. What are the results of making requests in non-assertive ways?

   - Last, journal about the times when you say "No" to an unreasonable request. Was it hard? Easy? How did you phrase your refusal? How did the other person react?

Suggestions for customizing the curriculum

1. For groups that you believe may struggle with the *Say the Alphabet* activity, the goal can be simplified into counting from 1 to 10 instead and/or hints can be given about how to organize members to achieve the task.

2. For groups less able to complete the reading or writing parts of the two handouts, consider doing the activities as a large group, with the facilitator reading the examples aloud and calling on volunteers to provide aggressive, passive, and assertive requests and refusals.

Handout: May I Please—Two Simple Rules for Making Assertive Requests

1. **State the request**

   This is not the time to be wordy or to volunteer extra information. Simply come right to the point and ask for what you need. For example:

   Will you please pick me up from school tomorrow?

2. **Be persistent**

   If you feel that your request is being ignored or put off, be persistent in asking for an answer. This does not mean that you will get an answer immediately, but it does mean that you will know when you can get an answer. For example:

   I need to know if you can pick me up by 7pm, so that I can tell Mrs. Weaver.

Copyright © Signe Whitson 2011

Activity: Write a Request

Based on the stated need, write a request according to each style:

Example:

1. **Help with homework**

   a. Passive request: (looking down) If you are not too busy, do you think you might be able to help me for just a minute or two with my homework if you don't mind?

   b. Aggressive request: It's your job to help me!

   c. Assertive request: Will you please help me with my math homework?

2. **Play a video game together**

   a. Passive request:

   b. Aggressive request:

   c. Assertive request:

3. **Payment of weekly allowance**

   a. Passive request:

   b. Aggressive request:

   c. Assertive request:

4. **Borrow a friend's clothing**

   a. Passive request:

   b. Aggressive request:

   c. Assertive request:

Copyright © Signe Whitson 2011

For discussion:

- *What are the problems with the passive and aggressive requests?*

- *Would you want someone to approach you using a passive or aggressive style?*

- *Do passive and aggressive styles make relationships better or worse? Explain.*

- *What is it about an assertive style that makes you more likely to get what you want?*

- *How does assertive communication build relationships?*

Copyright © Signe Whitson 2011

Handout: No Can Do—Four Rules for Refusing Requests Assertively

1. Be direct, firm, and honest when refusing a request.

   I prefer not to do that.

2. Ask for more information if you are not sure what the request involves.

   Can you tell me exactly how much time this project will involve?

3. Postpone giving an answer if you need more time to consider the request.

   I will need some time to think about that before I give you an answer. I will let you know by tomorrow afternoon.

4. Use I-Messages to express your feelings assertively if the other person tries to force you into granting their request.

   I feel frustrated when you continue to ask me the same question after I've given you my answer. I want you to take "no" for an answer and not make the same request repeatedly.

Copyright © Signe Whitson 2011

Activity: Passive, Aggressive, or Assertive?

Next to each statement, write whether the response is passive (P), aggressive (AG), or assertive (AS). If it is passive or aggressive, correct the statement to make it more assertive.

P	I don't think I should go because I have a headache and I don't have any money and I have to be home by 7pm anyway, but if you really need me to go, I'll go.	**No, I will not be able to go tonight.**
	No way will I let you wear my jeans. Every time I let you borrow something, it comes back dirty. And, you make it smell too!	
	I don't think I can help. Well, actually, I'm not sure. Call me later, if that's ok with you.	
	I won't be able to attend the meeting today.	
	I do not lend my sunglasses to others.	
	I hate all of your music. Why would I want to trade CDs with you?	
	I'm sick of people like you always wanting to go to the mall all the time.	
	I know I'm going to get in trouble for this, but I guess I'll go if you really want me to.	

Copyright © Signe Whitson 2011

For the facilitator: Suggested Answer Guide

P	I don't think I should go because I have a headache and I don't have any money and I have to be home by 7pm anyway, but if you really need me to go, I'll go.	**No, I will not be able to go tonight.**
AG	No way will I let you wear my jeans. Every time I let you borrow something, it comes back dirty. And, you make it smell too!	**No, I prefer not to lend my clothing.**
P	I don't think I can help. Well, actually, I'm not sure. Call me later, if that's OK with you.	**No, I can't help you this time.**
AS	No, I won't be able to attend the meeting today.	
AS	No, I do not lend my sunglasses to others.	
AG	I hate all of your music. Why would I want to trade CDs with you?	**No, I don't want to trade CDs.**
AG	I'm sick of people like you always wanting to go to the mall all the time.	**No, I prefer not to go to the mall.**
P	I know I'm going to get in trouble for this, but I guess I'll go if you really want me to.	**No, I cannot go with you.**

Copyright © Signe Whitson 2011

Handout: Assertive Dos and Don'ts of Saying "No"

Basic principle to follow: Be *brief, clear, firm,* and *honest* in responding to requests.

Do

1. Begin your answer with the word "no" to help make your response immediately clear.

2. Make your answers short and to the point.

3. Be honest, direct, and firm.

4. Use body language to support your refusal.

Don't

1. Give a long explanation for why you are saying no.

   - The more information you give, the more the requestor may try to refute your reasons.

   - The requestor may look as if he/she is waiting for more information about your refusal, but this does not mean you have to volunteer the information.

   - Maintain eye contact and assertive body language and learn to feel OK about saying "no" without a list of reasons.

2. Make excuses for why you are saying no.

   - It is your right to do so.

   - Excuses sound like apologies.

3. Say, "I'm sorry, but…"

   - This is not an apology; it is your assertive right to say "No" to a request you cannot reasonably meet.

Copyright © Signe Whitson 2011

Weekly journal

This week, take special note of the way that you, and those around you, approach asking for what you want and need. Practice making requests assertively and write or draw about the occasions that you did so.

Journal about the passive and aggressive requests that you observe in your day-to-day activities. What are the results of making requests in non-assertive ways?

Lastly, journal about the times when you say "no" to an unreasonable request. Was it hard? Easy? How did you phrase your refusal? How did the other person react?

Copyright © Signe Whitson 2011

✓

Notes for parents from Session 10

"May I Please" and "No Can Do:" Guidelines for Assertively Making and Refusing Requests

- Consider posting the *Two Simple Rules for Making Assertive Requests* and the *Four Rules for Refusing Requests Assertively* in your home, in a place where all family members can regularly read them and remind themselves often of the guidelines. Make it fun; younger kids can create colorful *May I Please* and *No Can Do* posters with simple craft materials.

- Many parents are accustomed to coaching their young children on using manners to make and refuse requests. Keep in mind that even older kids benefit from the consistent message that verbalizing their wants and needs is a healthy thing and that learning how to phrase requests and refusals in assertive terms is important.

- When situations arise in which your child is nervous or hesitant to make an important request, remind him/her of the two basic rules for making assertive requests and use role-play to help him/her learn to phrase the request effectively.

- Likewise, help your child rehearse and become comfortable with the skill of refusing requests assertively. The more you review the four rules for refusing requests assertively and practice the skills together, the easier it will be for your child to use assertive wording in a real-life situation.

Copyright © Signe Whitson 2011

"That's So Nice of You to Say"
Assertive Strategies for Giving and Receiving Compliments

Session objectives

- To review and practice skills for making and refusing requests assertively.
- To learn three rules for giving compliments assertively.
- To learn and practice six rules for assertively receiving compliments.

Materials needed

- index cards
- pencils or pens for participants to complete written activities
- flipchart paper and markers.

Before beginning

- Pre-print three rules for giving compliments assertively:
  ◦ Be vocal.
  ◦ Be sincere.
  ◦ Be specific.
- Pre-print the *Dos and Don'ts of Receiving Compliments Assertively* (page 166) on index cards.

- Prepare copies of the *Weekly journal* (page 168) for each participant.
- Prepare copies of the *Notes for parents* handout (page 169) for each participant to take home.

Welcome back

1. *Last week, we talked about overcoming the restraints of a passive style and being able to make and refuse requests assertively.*

2. *This week, we are going to revisit this topic with a little game, before moving on to our next skill.*

Putting It All Together: Making and Refusing Requests

1. Tell participants that the object of this activity is for each participant to gain practice making requests assertively and refusing requests assertively. They will practice these skills on each other.

2. Explain that for this activity, participants will be challenged to pull together many of the things they have learned in group so far, including using body language to communicate meaning, using I-Messages, and practicing the assertive skills of making and refusing requests.

    It may be helpful to do a two-minute review at this point, asking for a volunteer(s) to state the two guidelines for making assertive requests and another volunteer(s) to list the four rules for refusing requests assertively.

3. Participants should write down on an index card one object that is so personally valuable that they would not lend it to anyone for any reason. If a participant says no such thing exists, ask him to think of a rule or specific situation in which he would not lend the object (e.g. "I'm not allowed to lend my clothes").

4. Have participants form a single line (two lines will work if your group has more than ten people).

5. The person at the head of the line should face the rest of the line. When it is his turn, he should show his index card to the next person in line. That second person's job is to request to borrow the item listed on the first person's card. The first person's task is to assertively refuse the request.

    - First, the requestor should practice making the request using an assertive communication style.

- The person at the head of the line's task is to assertively, and persistently refuse the request, no matter what the requestor says or does.

- After two attempts using assertive phrasing, the requestor is free to use whatever style he wants, including using an aggressive voice, angry body language, etc.

6. The facilitator should carefully observe the activity and allow the back and forth to go on for a few rounds—enough to allow the first volunteer the chance to practice assertive refusal skills—but not so long that he gets flustered or frustrated.

7. Continue the activity until each participant has had the chance to make and refuse a request.

8. This activity is designed to give participants real practice in making and refusing requests. The facilitator should use his skill to make sure that this icebreaking/review activity is also enjoyable and provides the participants with a sense of learning and accomplishment.

9. For discussion:

   - *What did the second volunteer do effectively when it came to making an assertive request?*

   - *What did the first volunteer do well when it came to refusing the request?*

   - *What non-verbal behaviors were used to communicate feelings?*

   - *Were I-Messages used? If so, how?*

   - *What else did you note about the skills of assertively making and refusing requests?*

Giving Compliments

1. *Another mark of assertive, relationship-building communication is the ability to give and receive genuine compliments. This will be our main focus for today's session.*

2. Present these three essential rules for a good compliment:

   - Be vocal.

     ○ *The first thing to remember about good compliments is that they need to be spoken aloud.*

     ○ *Do not assume that someone knows that his clothes look good or that he did a good job in the baseball game.*

     ○ *Tell them in words!*

- Be sincere.
  - *If you say something just to "get on someone's good side," chances are, the person will pick up on your insincerity.*
  - *Since insincerity damages relationships, offer a compliment about something that is genuinely meaningful to you.*
  - *This can also help you find some things you enjoy in common with others, which is often the basis of good friendships!*

- Be specific.
  - *Compare these compliments:*
    - *Nice job!*
    - *I really like the way you helped Tim with his math. You were very patient and clear.*
  - *Which compliment conveys more information about what you liked? Which phrase is more likely to cause the behavior to occur again in the future?*

3. Ask for 2–3 participants to give examples of a compliment that follows all three rules. Affirm and clarify the examples.

Receiving Compliments

1. Ask for several volunteers who are willing to role-play some "Dos" and "Don'ts" for receiving compliments.

2. Give each volunteer an index card with a "Do" or a "Don't" for receiving a compliment.

3. Tell the volunteers that you will be giving them a compliment. Their job will be to receive the compliment according to the "Do" or "Don't" rule on their card.

   - The facilitator should be prepared to role model giving an assertive compliment to each volunteer. Choose something they have recently done well in group.

   - If volunteers have any questions about how they are to role-play their "Do" or "Don't" for receiving the compliment, they can ask you before the brief role-play.

4. Group members should be encouraged to discuss their observations of the role-play and to specify what went right/wrong with receiving the compliment.

5. After the role-plays and discussion are complete, give each participant a copy of the *Dos and Don'ts of Receiving Compliments* handout (page 166).

Session conclusion

1. *This week, we focused on giving and receiving compliments in an assertive style. It is a human need to receive positive feedback. Exchanging compliments helps strengthen relationships.*

2. *Next week, we'll revisit these skills and also talk about how to respond when someone else is expressing anger toward you. There are four sessions left of our group.*

3. Journal topic:

   • Each day, journal about one compliment you would like to give to someone else. Use the three rules as guidelines for giving a good compliment.

   • Now that you've thought through the guidelines, try offering the compliment to the person. How did he/she respond? How did giving a genuine compliment affect your relationship?

Suggestions for customizing the curriculum

   • Younger participants may struggle with the face-to-face nature of the opening activity. If necessary, the facilitator can set this activity up with participants working in pairs (instead of standing in line). Alternatively, the facilitator can play the role of the first volunteer and allow each participant to practice making requests, leaving the refusal task out of the activity.

   • The facilitator should adjust the language of the rules for *Giving and Receiving Compliments Assertively*, as necessary.

   • Younger participants may need more preparation time before presenting their role-plays in the *Dos and Don'ts of Receiving Compliments Assertively* activity. Older participants may be challenged to create their own role-plays or skits, based on the rules.

Handout: Dos and Don'ts of Receiving Compliments Assertively

1. Do accept the compliment with a simple "Thank you."

2. Do let the person know you appreciate the compliment:

   Thank you. I worked very hard and I really appreciate you noticing."

3. Do look the person in the eye when you acknowledge the compliment.

4. Do not reject the compliment by disagreeing with it. You may think you are being humble, but often your words accidentally insult the speaker and make you look ungrateful. It also makes people hesitate to compliment you in the future.

   If someone tells you your hair looks good, do not say, "Ugh, I'm having a bad hair day."

   If you are complimented on scoring during a sports match, do not say, "I totally messed up today—usually I score way more."

5. Do not shy away from the compliment by looking away, shrugging your shoulders, or giving the credit to someone else.

   Be proud of your personal strengths and acknowledge the compliment with confidence.

6. Do not discount the compliment by returning it right away. While it is always nice to compliment others, returning a compliment right away often sounds insincere. For example:

   Person 1: "I like your outfit."

   Person 2: "Thanks. I like yours too."

Copyright © Signe Whitson 2011

For the facilitator: Dos and Don'ts of Receiving Compliments Assertively

Use the statements below for the *Dos and Don'ts of Receiving Compliments Assertively* activity.

Prior to the session beginning, pre-print one "Do" or "Don't" on each index card and distribute to volunteers. Alternatively, make copies of this page and cut out the "Dos" and Don'ts".

Dos

- Accept the compliment with a simple "Thank you."
- Let the person know you appreciate the compliment.
- Look the person in the eye when you acknowledge the compliment.

Don'ts

- Reject the compliment by disagreeing with it.
- Discount the compliment by returning it right away.
- Shy away from the compliment by looking away, shrugging your shoulders, or giving the credit to someone else.

Copyright © Signe Whitson 2011

Weekly journal

Each day, journal about one compliment you would like to give to someone else. Use the three rules as guidelines for giving a good compliment.

Now that you've thought through the guidelines, try offering the compliment to the person. How did he/she respond? How did giving a genuine compliment affect your relationship?

Copyright © Signe Whitson 2011

Notes for parents from Session 11

"That's So Nice of You to Say:" Assertive Strategies for Giving and Receiving Compliments

- It is a human need to receive positive feedback and an important skill to communicate compliments to others. The best way to teach your child about how to give compliments assertively is to allow him/her to experience receiving affirmations often. When you speak sincere and specific compliments to your child, you strengthen your relationship and build his/her self-esteem.

- Ask your child to tell you about the three simple rules for giving good compliments (be vocal, be sincere, be specific.) Another creative poster or other family-wide reminder could be in order here! Practice makes perfect; make a daily appointment with your child in which you verbalize at least one sincere and specific compliment about something positive he/she does. Better yet, make it mutual. Encourage your child to practice giving good compliments to family members each day as well.

- Teach your child about how to receive a compliment, using the assertive rules outlined in this session. Use role-play to help develop his/her skills in receiving compliments assertively.

Copyright © Signe Whitson 2011

On the Receiving End
Four Steps for Responding Assertively to Anger

Session objectives

- To learn and practice four rules for responding to anger assertively.

Materials needed

- index cards
- pencils or pens for participants to complete written activities
- flipchart paper and markers.

Before beginning

- Pre-print the *Four Rules for Responding to Anger Assertively*:

  1. Listen openly.

  2. Avoid self-defeating anger styles.

  3. Use I-Messages.

  4. Practice coping skills.

- Prepare copies of the *Four Rules for Responding to Anger Assertively* handout (page 176) for each participant.

- (Optional) Pre-print the *Optional topics for Plays for Practicing the Skill of Responding to Anger Assertively* (page 177) on index cards.

- Prepare copies of the *Weekly journal* (page 178) for each participant.
- Prepare copies of the *Notes for parents* handout (page 179) for each participant to take home.

Welcome back

1. *Welcome back to our 12th session of this group. After today, we have three more sessions.*

2. Ask for volunteers to recall the various group topics and things they have learned in the group thus far. What stands out the most?

3. *Last week, we talked about how to give and receive compliments using an assertive style. This week, we'll practice this skill one more time before moving on to our next topic.*

Putting It All Together: Compliments

1. Arrange group members in a seated circle.

2. Ask for a volunteer(s) to list the three rules of giving a compliment (*be vocal, be sincere, be specific*).

3. Ask for additional volunteers to recall some of the *Dos and Don'ts* of receiving compliments.

4. Explain that in this first activity of the day, each participant will give a good compliment to the person sitting to their left. The recipient should practice accepting the compliment assertively. Then, he should turn to the person on his left and give him a good compliment. The activity should continue until everyone has had the chance to give and receive a compliment assertively.

5. After explaining the activity, allow 2–3 minutes for participants to think in advance about the wording of the sincere compliment they want to give to the person on their left. The facilitator should go first, to role model giving an assertive compliment.

6. For discussion:
   - *How did it feel to give an assertive compliment?*
   - *How did it feel to receive a sincere compliment?*
   - *How can the skill of giving and receiving compliments benefit you in your relationships?*

Responding to Anger

1. *Throughout our group sessions, we have been talking about our own anger, anger expression styles, and how to replace self-defeating anger expression styles with assertive behaviors.*

2. *Along with expressing anger assertively, it is also important to be able to respond assertively to others who are expressing anger toward you.*

3. Give each participant a copy of the *Four Rules for Responding to Anger Assertively* handout (page 176). Refer also to the abbreviated rules, pre-printed on the flipchart.

   - Listen openly.

   - Avoid self-defeating anger style.

   - Use I-Messages.

   - Practice coping skills.

4. Ask for a volunteer(s) to read each rule and explanation from the handout aloud.

5. Plan to spend 10–15 minutes going over the rules carefully, answering questions, clarifying statements, and asking for personal examples from the large group.

6. It may be especially useful to allow extra time to discuss (and even practice!) "Rule 4: Practice Coping Skills," as this is not a topic that has been specifically covered in the group.

7. Because of the histories of some of the kids in the group setting, there may be several who have been on the receiving end of dangerous, violent anger. Emphasize that the rules above apply when someone is expressing anger verbally. In situations of physical violence, the number one response should be seeking safety.

Plays for Practicing the Skill of Responding to Anger Assertively

1. Assign participants to work in pairs or groups of three to develop a quick play involving one person who is expressing verbal anger and the other who is responding assertively to the anger. Plays need only last for two minutes but should show the recipient of the anger using the rules above to respond assertively to anger.

2. Tell participants that although we have practiced the skill of expressing anger assertively, for the purposes of this play, all rules are off. Short of using personal attacks or insults, the "angry" participant can express anger in whatever verbal way he chooses, to give his partner the opportunity to practice maintaining assertive responses.

3. Encourage participants to build 3–4 exchanges between the "angry" person and the "responder" into their play.

4. Ask for at least 2–3 groups to present their plays to everyone.

5. For discussion:

    *   *How does it make you feel to have someone expressing anger toward you?*

    *   *What is the hardest thing about responding to anger?*

    *   *If someone is calling you names or insulting you personally, what is an assertive response?*

    *   *What skills have you learned in this group that will make it easier to respond effectively to someone's anger?*

Session conclusion

1. *This week, we focused on responding assertively when someone else is expressing anger toward you.*

2. *Next week, we will talk about finding win–win solutions to everyday problems.*

3. Journal topic:

    *   Write or draw about a time when you were the recipient of someone's verbal anger. How did it make you feel? How did you respond? Knowing what you know now, is there a different way you could choose to respond?

    *   There are no right or wrong answers to this activity. The purpose of this journaling task is to encourage you to reflect on assertive responses to someone else's anger.

Suggestions for customizing the curriculum

- For younger participants, take your time in teaching the *Four Rules for Responding to Anger Assertively*. Adjust the language and explanations to the appropriate level and provide examples for each rule to ensure that participants have a thorough understanding of the rules.

- If participants have difficulty thinking of their own topics for the *Plays for Practicing the Skill of Responding to Anger Assertively* activity, a list of optional topics is provided.

Handout: Four Rules for Responding to Anger Assertively

1. Listen openly.

- Pay attention to what the person is saying and seems to be feeling.
- Notice his/her body language and tone of voice.
- Show that you are listening through your body language.
- You can be attentive and tuned in to what the person is saying even if you do not agree with him/her.

2. Avoid self-defeating anger styles.

Passive: Don't run away from or ignore the anger, but rather let the person know in words that you know that he/she is angry. Most people care more that they are understood and that their feelings matter than they do about getting their own way.

Aggressive: Do not blame, shout, or insult the other person. These behaviors block good communication and cause others to become even angrier.

Passive aggressive: Avoid saying that you will do something, just to get the angry person to stop talking, but then not acting on your promise (*temporary compliance*). Be honest and genuine.

3. Use I-Messages to communicate your thoughts and feelings.

4. Practice coping skills.

Remember that your primary job in responding to anger is to practice your own coping skills. Soothe yourself with calming statements such as:

- *It's OK.*
- *Stay calm.*
- *Count to ten slowly.*
- *We can deal with this.*
- *Everyone is entitled to their own opinion.*

Copyright © Signe Whitson 2011

For the facilitator: Optional topics for Plays for Practicing the Skill of Responding to Anger Assertively

Pre-print these topics on index cards, for distribution to the participant who will be expressing anger:

1. You are angry that you are being left out of a football game. Express your anger.	2. You feel hurt that your friend shared a private email. Express your anger.
3. You feel angry that your student forgot his/her homework assignment— again! Express your anger..	4. You feel angry that your child did not clean up his/her room, after being reminded three times. Express your anger.
5. You feel angry that your toe was stomped on by a peer in the cafeteria line. Express your anger.	6. You feel angry that someone borrowed your DVD and returned it a week late— with a huge scratch on it! Express your anger.
7. You feel humiliated that your former best friend started an online rumor about you. Express your anger.	8. You feel angry that your friends left without you. Express your anger.
9. You feel hurt that your friend forgot to pick you up for soccer and you missed the game. Express your anger.	10. You feel angry because someone just knocked over your lunch tray. Express your anger.

Copyright © Signe Whitson 2011

Weekly journal

Write or draw about a time when you were the recipient of someone's verbal anger. How did it make you feel? How did you respond? Knowing what you know now, is there a different way you could choose to respond?

There are no right or wrong answers to this activity. The purpose of this journaling task is to encourage you to reflect on assertive responses to someone else's anger.

Copyright © Signe Whitson 2011

Notes for parents from Session 12

On the Receiving End: Three Steps for Responding Assertively to Anger

- In order for kids to believe that expressing their anger assertively is a valuable life skill, they must simultaneously experience that the adults who are close to them are willing and able to receive their anger. When parents role model assertive ways to respond to the anger that their kids are learning to express, they demonstrate both this willingness to accept honest self-expression and the skills with which to do it.

- Use real-world situations to discuss and practice with your child skills for responding to anger effectively.

- Reinforce that responding to someone else's anger does not mean that your child has to tolerate verbal attacks, insults, or abuse. When this type of anger is being expressed, your child can assert his/her right not to participate in the discussion or stand for the abuse. Refer your child back to the rules for standing up to bullies for guidelines on how to handle verbal abuse.

Copyright © Signe Whitson 2011

Four Square Problem-Solving
Finding Win–Win Solutions

Session objectives

- To understand the advantages of using a solution-focused mindset.
- To understand the relationship between assertiveness and problem-solving.
- To learn and utilize the Four Square method of problem-solving.

Materials needed

- flipchart paper and markers
- pencils or pens for participants to complete written activities.

Before beginning

- Pre-print these phrases on flipchart paper:
  - Developing a solution-focused mindset
  - "What can I do to make this better?"
  - Finding win–win solutions
- Prepare copies of the *Four Square Problem-Solving* handout (page 187).
- Prepare copies of the *Weekly journal* (page 188) for each participant.
- Prepare copies of the *Notes for parents* handout (page 189) for each participant to take home.

Welcome back

1. Welcome participants back to the group session. Begin with this re-cap of last week, asking participants to share what they wrote or drew in their weekly journals (participants do not have to read directly from their journals—a summary is fine):

   - *Was there a situation over the past week in which you had to face someone else's anger over something you said or did?*

   - *What was the situation?*

   - *How did you respond?*

   - *What was helpful about the way you responded?*

   - *Is there anything you wish you had done differently?*

2. *Learning to use assertive communication skills in our daily lives is not a skill that happens overnight, but rather one that requires practice and consistent use. Over time, assertive words and body language begin to be a part of your natural style.*

3. *What's more, you will begin to notice that your use of assertive communication changes the way that others interact with you. Knowing that you will not respond with aggressive, passive, or passive aggressive behaviors, people will tend to respond to you in more fair, rational, direct ways.*

4. *As part of your ongoing journal, take note of the occasions when your assertive responses seem to change the way others are approaching you and/or seem to help you achieve your goals.*

5. *Today, we are going to talk about a method of problem-solving that can help you when you are at odds with someone else. Rather than experiencing anger over competing needs, this method puts you and the other person on the same team, working together to agree upon win–win solutions.*

Four Square Problem-Solving

1. Tell the group that we are going to begin this session by talking about problems and end it by developing solutions. The focus of this group session will be on *developing a solution-focused mindset*.

2. Point out the pre-printed flipchart with the phrases "Developing a solution-focused mindset," "What can I do to make this better?" and "Finding win–win solutions."

3. Read the following scenario to participants:

   Jake asks his mother if he can use the computer to play his favorite game. His sister, Emily, says, "No way, Jake. I need to do research on the computer for my school project that's due on Friday. If you get on that computer, you'll hog it all night long."

4. Ask participants to brainstorm possible solutions to Jake and Emily's competing needs.

   - Record each idea on flipchart paper.

   - It may be effective to allow a participant volunteer to stand at the front with you to record the answers. Be sure to pick a volunteer who can write quickly and clearly enough for everyone to read.

   - If participants are excessively even-minded about this, make sure to suggest unbalanced solutions that favor either Jake or Emily. Add all of the ideas to the list.

5. Once a list of at least 5–10 solutions have been generated, congratulate participants on their ability to generate solutions to a problem.

6. Tell participants that an important *solution* to feelings of overwhelming anger is to adopt a mindset that is focused on finding *win–win solutions*.

7. *Rather than staying focused on a problem, assertive people consistently ask themselves, "What can I do to make this situation better?"*

8. *Four Square problem-solving is a method participants can use to take any situation in which there are competing needs and develop win–win solutions through which both people's needs can be met.*

9. Using the writing space in the front of the room, the facilitator should sketch out the following diagram:

Emily's needs

	Win–Win	Win–Lose
Jake's needs	Win–Win	Win–Lose
	Lose–Win	Lose–Lose

10. Challenge participants to categorize each of the ideas that were brain-stormed earlier into one of the four squares.

11. A sample completed Four Square for Jake and Emily's problem may resemble the following:

Emily's needs

	Win–Win	Win–Lose
Jake's needs	• Jake uses the computer for 30 minutes, then Emily gets a turn for 30 minutes. • Emily uses the computer first to complete her research, then Jake gets the computer for an equal amount of time afterwards. • Emily uses the computer tonight since it is for school. Jake gets extra computer game time over the weekend. • Jake and Emily create a sign-up list for the computer in the future, and schedule time that it will be needed for schoolwork.	• Jake asked for permission to use the computer first, so he gets to play.
	Lose–Win	**Lose–Lose**
	• Emily gets to use the computer since she needs it for schoolwork, which is more important than a game.	• If Jake and Emily can't agree upon a compromise, they both lose their computer privileges for the night.

12. After each possible solution has been categorized, encourage discussion about the process:

- *Most problems have win–win solutions, so long as both parties are willing to adopt a solution-focused mindset and accept compromise.*

- *Since assertiveness is all about standing up for your own wants and needs without violating the wants and needs of others, Four Square problem-solving is an important tool that represents a win for all.*

> • *Moreover, when two people with competing needs adopt the common mindset of finding win–win solutions, they often find that their needs don't have to be in opposition and their anger at one another tends to lessen.*

Putting It All Together

1. Give each participant a copy of the *Four Square Problem-Solving* handout (page 187).

2. Assign participants to work in pairs or groups of three to use the Four Square method to work through a real-world problem.

3. Challenge participants to come up with 6–8 total solutions and at least two win–win solutions.

4. Allow 5–10 minutes for the small groups to work on their problem, and then invite each group to present their scenario and their completed Four Square.

5. If time permits, encourage the small groups to create a brief play out of their scenario, acting out each possible solution and showing the various outcomes.

6. Encourage group discussion about each Four Square presentation, with questions such as:

   • *What do you think about the solutions that were identified?*

   • *How do lose–lose solutions impact a relationship between two people?*

   • *How do lose–win / win–lose solutions impact relationships?*

   • *What is the effect of win–win solutions on a relationship?*

   • *Are the win–win solutions fair and balanced?*

   • *Will each person be able to have their need met?*

7. In your own words, convey the following summary points:

   • *Many conflicts arise out of competing needs.*

   • *An important aspect of assertiveness is that people are able to express and exercise their needs without violating the needs of others.*

   • *The Four Square problem-solving method helps people with competing needs maintain a solution-focused mindset.*

   • *Instead of becoming overwhelmed with anger, assertive people seek to find win–win solutions, using the Four Square method, to find common ground.*

Session conclusion

1. *Today, we talked about developing a solution-focused mindset and looking for win–win solutions to everyday problems.*

2. *Next week, we will take one last look at some of the self-defeating patterns we've discussed during our group sessions and make a commitment to replacing those behaviors with our newly developed assertiveness skills.*

3. Journal topic:

   - This week, take time to think about the conflicts in your life and in the lives of those around you. Do many of the disagreements and anger-inspiring conflicts have to do with competing needs? Write or draw examples of the conflicts you experience and observe.

   - Use the Four Square problem-solving method to think through a conflict of competing needs. What win–win solutions can you think of? If utilized, how might these solutions impact the relationship between the people in the conflict?

Suggestions for customizing the curriculum

- Younger participants may benefit from practicing additional Four Squares as a group before continuing on to develop their own original scenario.

- During the *Putting It All Together* small group activity, some participants may struggle with developing their own real-world situation. The facilitator should provide relevant examples for participants to consider or coach participants in thinking about an appropriate problem-situation from their own lives.

Handout: Four Square Problem-Solving

Think of a real-world problem or conflict involving competing needs. In pairs or small groups, develop as many solutions as possible to the problem.

Be sure to come up with at least two win–win solutions.

Situation:

Win–Win	Win–Lose
Lose–Win	**Lose–Lose**

Copyright © Signe Whitson 2011

✓

Weekly journal

This week, take time to think about the conflicts in your life and in the lives of those around you. Do many of the disagreements and anger-inspiring conflicts have to do with competing needs? Write or draw examples of the conflicts you experience and observe.

Use the Four Square problem-solving method to think through a conflict of competing needs. What win–win solutions can you think of? If utilized, how might these solutions impact the relationship between the people in the conflict?

Copyright © Signe Whitson 2011

Notes for parents from Session 13

Four Square Problem-Solving: Finding Win–Win Solutions

- Ask your child to share with you the *Four Square Problem-Solving* handout from the group and explain how he/she completed the activity.

- This easy-to-use method can be a great tool for family members of all ages to use together to develop a solution-focused mindset and win–win solutions to real problems. Practice using this technique with imagined problems so that children are well versed in the mindset and process of finding win–win solutions.

- Whenever possible, emphasize to kids that instead of becoming overwhelmed with anger, assertive people seek to find win–win solutions.

Copyright © Signe Whitson 2011

Part III
Committing to Assertive Anger Expression

What's the Plan?
Replacing Self-Defeating Patterns and Committing to Assertive Behaviors

Session objectives

- To understand the behaviors that represent the four choices in anger expression.
- To identify differences between self-defeating patterns and assertive behaviors.
- To commit in writing to replacing self-defeating patterns with assertiveness skills.

Materials needed

- index cards
- flipchart paper and markers
- pencils or pens for participants to complete written activities.

Before beginning

- Prepare index cards for the *Complete the Sentence* activity (page 201).
- Pre-print the four anger expression styles on flipchart paper and hang in distinct areas of the room:

- ◦ passive
- ◦ aggressive
- ◦ passive aggressive
- ◦ assertive.

- Prepare copies of *My Plan—Replacing Self-Defeating Patterns and Committing to Assertive Behaviors* handout (page 203).

- Prepare copies of the *Weekly journal* (page 205) for each participant.

- Prepare copies of the *Notes for parents* handout (page 206) for each participant to take home.

Welcome back

1. Welcome participants back to the group. Provide this brief review:

   a. *Last week, we talked about using the Four Square problem-solving method as a way of developing a solution-focused mindset.*

   b. Ask: *What does being solution-focused have to do with assertiveness?*

   Answer:

   - *Assertiveness has everything to do with getting our needs met without violating the rights and needs of others.*

   - *When we adopt a solution-focused mindset, we seek to find win–win solutions that satisfy the needs of both persons.*

   - *Win–win solutions also help prevent the overwhelming anger that leads to aggressive, passive, and/or passive aggressive behaviors.*

   c. *Did anyone face a situation over the past week in which there was a conflict over competing needs? What were the Four Square options? How was the conflict resolved? Was this an effective resolution? How was the relationship impacted?*

2. *Today, we are going to talk once more about the four choices in anger expression and use our new knowledge to revisit an old list we made, back in Session 2.*

3. *As we prepare to end this assertive anger expression group and move forward with the skills you have gained, each participant will write down a plan for replacing old, self-destructive anger expression patterns and committing to new assertive behaviors.*

Icebreaker activity: Complete the Sentence

1. Arrange the participants in a seated circle.

2. Tell group participants that before we talk about our four choices in anger expression, we're going to play a quick game. We've spent 13 group sessions getting to know each other's anger expression styles. Now, we're going to get to know some fun information about each other by playing *Complete the Sentence.*

3. Give each participant a card from the *Complete the Sentence* activity (page 201).

4. Tell participants that group members will be taking turns, sharing their answers to the phrase on their card.

5. Emphasize that this is intended as a fun, light-hearted activity.

6. The facilitator should go first to role model the activity.

   For example, if the facilitator picks the "superpowers" card, he might simply say, "If I could have any superpower, I would be able to fly."

7. Continue until all participants have had a chance to complete their sentence.

Choices in Anger Expression

1. *Recall that back when we first began this assertive anger expression group, we defined anger. Can anyone remember the key parts of our definition of anger?*

   Facilitator should affirm responses that include any of the following elements:

   - Anger is a real, powerful, natural emotion, usually triggered by frustration.
   - Anger comes and goes and can be experienced as mild, medium, and intense.

2. *We also talked about four basic anger expression styles and choices that we all have when it comes to expressing our anger. Name the four styles:*

   - aggressive
   - passive aggressive
   - passive
   - assertive.

3. *Today, we are going to brainstorm a list of the behaviors that people use to express anger and follow it up with a discussion of which behaviors help us achieve our goals vs. which obstruct our goals and defeat our needs.*

Step 1

1. Using flipchart paper, the facilitator should challenge participants to name as many anger expression behaviors as they can think of.

   - Tying in the *Complete the Sentence* activity, it might help to write a heading such as, "When I am angry, I…".

   - Both self-defeating and assertive behaviors should be included in the brainstorming. The facilitator should record all responses.

   - At this point in the group, participants should have no problem generating answers.

   - If the group is slow getting started, however, or leaves out key behaviors, the facilitator should help out with examples such as:

     ○ hit, punch, kick, spit, etc. (AG)

     ○ curse (AG)

     ○ compliment the person after he has insulted you (P)

     ○ apologize even if it is not your fault (P)

     ○ run away (P)

     ○ start/spread a rumor (PA)

     ○ get others to gang up on the person (PA)

     ○ give the person the silent treatment (PA)

     ○ make direct eye contact (AS)

     ○ ask an adult for help solving the conflict (AS)

     ○ talk it out (AS)

     ○ use I-Messages (AS).

AG=Aggressive, AS=Assertive, PA=Passive Aggressive, P=Passive

Step 2

1. After the brainstorming part of the exercise is complete (aim for at least 10–15 behaviors), divide the participants into four groups, assigning each one a particular anger expression style.

2. Give each group a marker. Using the list that was just brainstormed, small group members should select the behaviors that fit into their assigned style, and write those behaviors on their flipchart.

3. The facilitator should provide guidance, as necessary.

Step 3

1. When the groups have completed Step 2, pose this question to all participants:

   When you are feeling angry, which of these behaviors help you accomplish your overall goals? Which behaviors stand in your way?

2. The "obvious" answer to the question is that the behaviors on the assertive list are most effective in helping participants stand up for their rights and needs without violating the rights of others. When this answer is offered by a participant, follow up by asking:

   How do assertive behaviors help you achieve your goals?

3. Indicate to participants that the group will be making another list to offer multiple answers to the question.

4. Offer a participant the opportunity to record the answers on the flipchart paper.

5. Encourage responses such as assertive behaviors:

   - build relationships
   - allow for win–win solutions
   - stop bullying
   - express genuine thoughts and feelings.

6. It may be very instructive for the facilitator to briefly play the role of devil's advocate by posing this rhetorical question:

   Isn't it true that aggressive, passive, and passive aggressive behaviors also help you achieve your goals? After all, in the moment, hitting someone, apologizing even if it is not your fault, or spreading a rumor may all be effective methods of revenge or stopping the problem.

7. It is important for the facilitator to acknowledge that the ways participants have expressed anger in the past are all ways that worked in the *short term*.

8. In the long term, however, aggressive, passive, and passive aggressive behaviors have had significant costs for each participant, including:

    -   damaged relationships

    -   loss of privileges

    -   school suspensions

    -   undesired consequences

    -   loss of trust.

    (The facilitator should write these down, as a contrast to the benefits that can be gained from using assertive behaviors.)

Step 4

1. Affirm that group members have been working very hard over the last 14 sessions to learn about anger expression styles and to practice assertive behaviors. They are on a road to replacing old, self-destructive patterns with new assertive behaviors and as the last activity for the day they will be committing to these new behaviors in writing.

2. Give each participant a copy of the *My Plan—Replacing Self-Defeating Patterns and Committing to Assertive Behaviors* handout (page 203).

3. Assign each participant to work individually to write down a personal action plan.

4. Tell participants that during the next session, you will be giving them back one copy of their plan, and keeping one copy for yourself. Even though the group will be ending soon, the action plan will be ongoing. In a few months, you will be following up with each participant to check on how they are doing and their commitment to replacing self-destructive patterns with new assertive behaviors.

5. Facilitators should collect all copies of the completed plans. When the session is over, prepare photocopies as described, one for returning to participants next week and one for safeguarding for a period of three months.

6. Mark your calendars: three months from the end date of the assertive anger expression group, the facilitator should follow up with each group participant, as promised, using the *How Is It Going? Replacing Self-Destructive Patterns and Committing to Assertive Behaviors* letter template (page 204).

7. This follow-up piece is an important way of connecting the assertive anger expression group experience to the real lives of participants. The letter serves as an important reminder to participants that:

   • each person is accountable for applying the lessons learned in group to their everyday lives

   • the facilitator cares about their well-being and wants them to succeed beyond the scope of the group sessions.

   Please note: Facilitators should never contact group participants at their homes, through social networking, text message, or any other personal contact that violates the boundaries of a professional relationship with a former group participant. The "check-in" letter should be delivered through professional channels only, such as in school or within a therapeutic or youth organization. Further, the letter should only be individualized with the child's name and stated goals, but should not include any other personal information or communication.

8. The facilitator should make a priority of this follow-up action; participants will be waiting and wondering if you care enough to hold them accountable in this way.

Session conclusion

1. *There is one final group session to go.*

2. *Today, each of you made a commitment to use all that you have learned.*

3. *Next week, we will review all of the lessons of the group and honor the hard work that each of you has done.*

4. Journal topic:

   • Think about the plan you wrote down for *Replacing Self-Destructive Patterns and Committing to Assertive Behaviors.* Over the course of the week, notice if there are any situations that require your sticking to the plan. What are they? Were you able to use assertive behaviors? Was it a challenge? What were the reactions of others? What benefits did you enjoy from using assertive behaviors? What costs did you avoid?

Suggestions for customizing the curriculum

- In Steps 1 and 2 of the *Choices in Anger Expression* activity, younger participants may need help generating ideas and properly categorizing different anger behaviors. The facilitator should provide assistance as necessary.

- Older participants may be able to handle Steps 1 and 2 with greater independence. Consider allowing participants to work in pairs or groups of three to complete these steps.

- Step 3 should be done as a group, with the facilitator taking care to offer the guidance that is needed, according to participant abilities.

- Offer one-on-one support to those who need it to complete *My Plan* in Step 4.

Activity: Complete the Sentence

For the facilitator

- Prior to beginning the session, cut out each sentence starter below (or copy each phrase onto an index card).

- Be sure to prepare enough statements for each group member.

- It may be helpful to have a few extra statements prepared, in case any participants prefer not to answer the statement they are given.

- You may also choose to create your own sentence starters, to fit the tone and abilities of the group.

If I could have any superpower, it would be…
I am good at…
My favorite thing to do in my free time is…
I like to collect…
When I was younger, my favorite thing to play was…
People say that I look like…
Someday, I would love to visit…
In the future, I would love to travel to…
My favorite candy is…

Copyright © Signe Whitson 2011

I love to watch movies about…

My favorite style of music is…

If I had to choose between ice cream, cookies, or cake, I would choose…

If I was given one million dollars, I would…

When I am with my best friend, I feel…

One positive change I have made recently is that…

One thing that makes me feel proud of myself is…

A motto that I like to live by is…

The most supportive person in my life is…

To me, an ideal friend is one who…

One goal that I have for the next year is to…

At first I was nervous about _____, but once I tried it, it was great!

When I feel stressed out, I…

I am always losing my…

I am always forgetting to…

Copyright © Signe Whitson 2011

Handout: My Plan—Replacing Self-Defeating Patterns and Committing to Assertive Behaviors

Real, lasting change does not happen overnight. It takes time and practice to break old habits and start using new ones. You have been working very hard over the last 14 sessions to learn about anger expression styles and practice assertive behaviors. You are on the road to replacing old, self-defeating patterns with new assertive behaviors. Congratulations on all of your hard work!

Use this worksheet to make a plan for to using assertive behaviors outside of the group and in your everyday life.

In the past when I have felt angry, I have expressed my anger by:

This pattern created problems for me, however, including:

Instead of continuing along this pathway, I will replace self-defeating patterns with assertive behaviors. Three specific skills that I learned in this group and will commit to using in my everyday life include:

1.

2.

3.

Participant signature_____ Date _____

Copyright © Signe Whitson 2011

✓

Letter template: How Is It Going? Replacing Self-Defeating Patterns and Committing to Assertive Behaviors

Facilitator,

Please use your own handwritten or typed words to send a "check-in" letter to each of your former assertive anger expression group participants, three months after the conclusion of the group. The text below provides a general template of the intended tone of the letter.

Please note: Facilitators should never contact group participants at their homes, through social networking, text message, or any other personal contact that violates the boundaries of a professional relationship with a former group participant. This "check-in" letter should be delivered through professional channels only, such as in school or within a therapeutic or youth organization. Further, the letter should only be individualized with the child's name and stated goals, but should not include any other personal information or communication.

Dear <u>Participant's name</u>,

It has been three months since we concluded our assertive anger expression group. In this time, I hope you have been practicing new assertive skills in your everyday life. During one of our last group sessions, you wrote an Action Plan (copy attached) in which you committed to replacing self-defeating patterns with relationship-strengthening assertive behaviors. You committed to using these three skills in your everyday life:

1.

2.

3.

I am writing to check in with you to see how you are progressing with your goals. Remember, change does not happen overnight, but the more you practice assertive behaviors, the more natural they will feel. I hope you have stayed committed to practicing these and other assertive behaviors and I encourage you to continue to be assertive in your everyday interactions. I believe in you and I know you can do it!

Sincerely,

<u>Facilitator's name</u>

Copyright © Signe Whitson 2011

Weekly journal

Think about the plan you wrote for *Replacing Self-Destructive Patterns and Committing to Assertive Behaviors*. Over the course of the week, notice if there are any situations that require your sticking to the plan. What are they? Were you able to use assertive behaviors? Was it a challenge? What were the reactions of others? What benefits did you enjoy from using assertive behaviors? What costs did you avoid?

Copyright © Signe Whitson 2011

Notes for parents from Session 14

What's the Plan? Replacing Self-Defeating Patterns and Committing to Assertive Behaviors

- Use everyday situations to spark discussions with your child about the different choices that people make to express their anger. Ask your child to consider which choices help people achieve their overall goals (improved relationships, honest self-expression, win–win solutions, etc.) and which are self-defeating. Regular discussions about choices in anger expression prepare kids to make positive choices when coping with their anger.

- Help your child commit to replacing self-defeating behaviors with assertiveness skills by developing an action plan. Post the plan in a visible location, where your child can be reminded often of his/her commitment. Be sure to hold your child accountable to his/her plan through gentle reminders and affirmations.

Copyright © Signe Whitson 2011

Putting It All Together
Choosing to Use Assertive Behaviors to Express Anger

Session objectives

- To understand the behaviors that represent the four choices in anger expression.

- To identify differences between self-defeating patterns and assertive behaviors.

- To commit in writing to replacing self-defeating patterns with assertiveness skills.

Materials needed

- large poster board

- markers

- scissors

- pencils or pens for participants to complete written activities.

Before beginning

- Prepare copies of the *Assertive Anger Expression* handout (page 210) for each participant.

- For the *Group Puzzle* activity, using marker(s), write, "We will choose to use assertive behaviors to express anger" across the large poster board. Then, cut the poster board into 20 or more pieces—2–3 per participant is ideal.

- Prepare copies of the *Participant Evaluation Form* (page 213) for each participant.

- Prepare copies of a *Certificate of Completion* (page 214) for each participant.
- Prepare copies of the *Notes for parents* handout (page 215) for each participant to take home.

Welcome back

1. Remind participants that this is the 15th and final session of this group.

2. Let participants know that you are interested in their feedback and will give them a chance both to verbalize and to express in writing what they liked and disliked about the assertive anger expression group as well as suggestions for future group sessions.

Icebreaker activity: Assertive Anger Expression

1. Challenge the group members to work together to complete the *Assertive Anger Expression* handout (page 210), based on the topics covered in group.

2. Congratulate the group on how well they've participated and how much they've learned and grown over the past 15 weeks.

3. If possible, offer group members a group small treat or reward when they successfully complete and turn in their *Assertive Anger Expression* paper.

Group Puzzle

1. Tell the group that over the last 15 weeks, each person shared a lot and learned a lot about self-defeating styles of anger expression. Participants have also learned new skills and alternatives to old, troublesome behaviors.

   - *There is a lot that you will "take with you" from the group, but perhaps the most important lesson of all was how group members came together, worked together and learned together.*

   - *For the final activity, the group is going to work together to solve a puzzle.*

   - *During each session of this group, you shared experiences and answers that made the group meaningful. The same will happen now as you work together to assemble a puzzle.*

   - *Only with everyone's unique contribution will the puzzle be complete and the message become clear.*

2. Distribute puzzle pieces to each participant. Assign the participants to put their pieces together to form a group message.

3. When the puzzle is fully assembled, ask participants to read the sentence aloud, in unison.

Feedback

1. Emphasize to participants that their feedback about the group experience is important.

2. Arrange participants in a seated circle and ask for a volunteer to begin by saying the most important thing they learned in group and their favorite group activity. The person to their left should then say the same information aloud, and so on until all group members have commented.

3. Following the circle activity, ask each participant to complete the written *Participant evaluation form.* Assure participants that they can choose to/not to put their name on the form.

Conclusion

1. Summarize group learning and accomplishments and reassure group members that you view the experience, their learning, and their participation as a success.

2. Collect forms and hand out a *Certificate of Completion* to each group member.

3. Wish the group well in using what they learned from the group.

Suggestions for customizing the curriculum

• Younger participants may have difficulty completing the *Assertive Anger Expression* handout. The facilitator can participate in this activity as much or as little as needed to help participants complete all of the responses successfully.

• If younger participants have difficulty with written feedback, they can be offered the chance to share the feedback with the facilitator or another adult who can relay the feedback to the facilitator.

✓

Handout: Assertive Anger Expression

Over the last 15 sessions, you have learned a great deal about anger expression and assertiveness. Use this new knowledge to answer the questions below.

Answer any 8 of the 12 questions below, and then give your completed paper to the facilitator.

1. The four anger expression styles:

   a.

   b.

   c.

   d.

2. Name one way that your body language shows assertiveness:

3. The "formula" for constructing an I-Message:

4. The five levels of passive aggressive behavior:

   a.

   b.

   c.

   d.

   e.

Copyright © Signe Whitson 2011

5. How do bullies try to make their victims feel?

6. The four rules for standing up to bullies assertively:

   a.

   b.

   c.

   d.

7. The two rules for making assertive requests:

   a.

   b.

8. The four rules for refusing requests assertively:

   a.

   b.

   c.

   d.

Copyright © Signe Whitson 2011

9. The three rules of giving good compliments:

    a.

    b.

    c.

10. The Dos and Don'ts of receiving compliments:

11. The four rules of responding to anger:

    a.

    b.

    c.

    d.

12. What do win–win solutions have to do with assertiveness?

Copyright © Signe Whitson 2011

Handout: Participant Evaluation Form

What did you like best about this group?

Was there a specific activity or discussion that you thought was really good?

What could be done to improve this group?

What is the most important thing you learned in this group?

Name (optional): _____

Copyright © Signe Whitson 2011

Handout: Certificate of Completion

This is to certify that

....

has successfully completed the

Assertive Anger Expression Group

from ___/___/___   to   ___/___/___

at

....

Signed:

....

Copyright © Signe Whitson 2011

Notes for parents from Session 15

Putting It All Together: Choosing to Use Assertive Behaviors to Express Anger

- Endings can be difficult for kids. As the assertive anger expression group comes to a close, affirm your child's successful participation and learning. If the friendships formed in the group will continue (i.e. through in-school relationships), affirm the ongoing nature of the bond that was formed and the continuing support your child will have to practice new behaviors.

- Continue using real-life situations to spark discussions about choices in anger expression and to develop your child's assertiveness skills through role-plays and rehearsal.

Copyright © Signe Whitson 2011

References

Brendtro, L., Mitchell, M. and McCall, H. (2009) *Deep Brain Learning: Pathways to Potential with Challenging Youth*. Albion, MI: Circle of Courage Institute and Starr Commonwealth.

Long, N., Long, J. and Whitson, S. (2009) *The Angry Smile: The Psychology of Passive Aggressive Behavior in Families, Schools, and Workplaces*, 2nd edn. Austin, TX: Pro-ED, Inc.

Shulman, L. (2008) *The Skills of Helping Individuals, Families, Groups and Communities*, 6th edn. Belmont, CA: Brooks/Cole.

Smead, R. (1995) *Skills and Techniques for Group Work with Children and Adolescents*. Champaign, IL: Research Press.

Whitson, S. (2012) *Friendship and Other Weapons: Group Activities to Help Young Girls Aged 5–11 to Cope with Bullying*. London: Jessica Kingsley Publishers.